The Flower Girl

Hidden

JOYCE J. MOORE

Kingdom J'Moore Publishing LLC

Credits

Edited by Ada's Art Inc.
Writing Consultants
H. Faye Clemmons, Darlene Moore &
LaDrena D. Henderson
Book Cover Design
Joyce A. Starks-Moore & Benjamin Garrett

Dedication

To all who have experienced abuse and trauma in the form of incest, molestation, rape, mental or physical abuse, drugs, alcohol, or suicide attempts. If your experience happened many years ago or whether you are currently in an abusive situation and you feel you have no control and no way out, I want to offer you hope. I can identify with your pain and the feelings of helplessness and hopelessness. The struggle is real. My prayer is that sharing my journey somehow will help to change and bring transformation to your life.

I would like to take you on a chronological journey of my life as an abused victim to the victorious woman God always intended me to be. Unfortunately, but very respectfully, I believe my life is a mirror of someone else's story. However, I overcame the demons that haunted me daily, and you can too. It doesn't matter whether it happened this week or 30 years ago, God can give you the release you need with added peace and joy you never even dreamed possible. You are the *hidden flower* of God who will blossom to be the person you were created to be, with purpose designed by God Almighty. There is a season for your freedom. *NOW!*

Seasons of Life

Acknowledgements

I would like to acknowledge the people who helped me through my journey and contributed to my escape, my rescue, my healing, and my deliverance. I am amazed and forever grateful for each of their assignments in my life. Many of them are now deceased; however, never will I forget how God used each one as an angelic presence in my journey to divine healing, purpose, and victory.

My mother, Aliece Moore, Aunt/mother Berniece Rudd, Grandparents B. J. & Lucy Rawls, Aunt Flossie & Uncle J. C. Ligon, Aunt Pike, Aunt Kay Mann, Ruby "Jean" Mauldin, Jerry Ligon, Saul Simpson, Reginald Kimbell, Jr., William "Billy" Poole, Michael Thompson aka "Mellow Mike," Debra Thompson, Larry Demps, Starlet Ellis Brown, Lydia Peer, David Peer, Willie Brooks, Helen Evans, Jesse Huggins, Venita Burns, Faye Clemmons, Joyce Starks-Moore, Betty Wright, Ann Mack, Carmen Moore, brother & former Pastor Garry Moore, LaVerne Butler, Norman Pearsall, Betty Pearsall, Fontaine Lasley, my adopted dad Walter Lott, Linda Pratt, Cindy Hale, Roma Kye, David Kye, Billie Shipp, Donald Shipp, Poletha Webster, Glynis Smith, Jacqueline Price, Jesse & Earlene "Honey" Hopson, Maxine Ballard, Virginia Hill-Shannon, Charles "Cary" Hill, Alvin Miles, Marilyn Shipp-Gary, Darlene Moore, Aletha Thomas, Leo C. Thompson, Jr., my son LeMario D. Thompson (my greatest miracle and blessing!), Antoinette Cecilia Beasley, former pastors: Bishop David Ellis, Bishop Henry & Prophetess Patricia Phillips, and Apostle Eddie L. Long.

Forward

Lady Joyce Starks-Moore

As long as I can remember there has always been *Joyce Jean Moore* in my life. We were literally born in the church; "Church Babies" or "Pew Babies" (if you will) raised in the "Sanctified" Church, the *Apostolic Faith Pentecostal Church* to be exact. We grew up in a small town where everybody knows everybody.

Joyce's grandparents were pillars in the church and the community. They were my mother's *godparents*, which caused our moms to become *god sisters*. The connection was indeed a God connection; we are family forever. To this very day, I refer to Joyce's grandparents (Daddy B & Mama Lucy) as being the grandparents I never had. They poured so, so much love into us, the church, the community, and anyone in need. Their home was an open door to many; it was our hang out spot.

We had countless Sunday dinners there. The house was always full of family and friends, and I can't forget the aroma that filled it from Mama Lucy's good cooking! Those were the good ole' days. We would play 'church' and mimic what we saw the adults do when praising the Lord. We would nearly "destroy" Mama Lucy's living room with her "good" pots, pans and utensils because those were our instruments. I could never just "play church" because I would always get serious and (in today's term) truly "catch the Holy Ghost" every time. UGH! SMH! LOL! *(SMH means Shaking my head, LOL means laughing out loud)*

Singing and playing our imaginary instruments became our reality, for our entire family can sing and or play an instrument: Joyce on piano or organ, her brothers on their guitars, and her sisters are singers in their own right.

Daddy B & Mama Lucy truly had evidence of the love of God in their hearts; they treated Mother, my siblings, and I like their very own. We were raised as *family* and as we grew up, only our heads knew there was NO DNA connection. . . our hearts didn't know the difference. The love we share is real!

Growing up I remember Joyce being a good child, seldom getting in any trouble. She was a very mild-mannered child, always respectful to her parents and other adults. Being the oldest of five, I can remember Joyce's grandfather often saying with pride that she was the "best-mannered" child her mom had out of her siblings. She got good grades in school. Never sassy, NOT spoiled! Just an overall good kid, indeed a good big sister.

Joyce loves music. I know now that music provided an escape from her reality; it was her safe place. For years, she was the church organist. And her brothers formed a singing group called "The Mighty Bells of Joy." They did very well for many years and were popular within our circle.

In retrospect, I see that Joyce was crying out for help. She was always sick, always expressing how she did not feel well. Something was wrong, for she was always in pain and crying a lot, especially in church services. SO much SO that, unfortunately, Joyce was being taken for granted. Many times, she was looked at as wanting attention. Truth be told, Joyce was living her worst nightmare. She was living in a bubble, screaming for help, BUT very few heard her. The only way she could express her pain was to be disruptive in a service, which drew temporary attention BUT NOT the healing she SO DESPERATELY NEEDED!

I have watched and witnessed many stages of her life: the struggle, the secrets, the hurt, the guilt, and the shame. BUT thanks be to GOD, He has turned her mourning into dancing, her sorrow into JOY! Her embarrassment has become empowerment and GOD has given her His Peace in her chaos!

This book is only the beginning of many to come. I am SO godly proud of the woman YOU have become, Joyce. In spite of everything you've endured, it has worked for your good! You are standing stronger than ever with a testimony of GOD'S healing and restoration, and I'm rejoicing for and with you! This book will bless nations.

Ladies & Gentlemen, Brothers & Sisters! It is my happy privilege to introduce what was already predestined: my god sister forever ◇future New York Times Best Sellers' list author, Joyce Jean Moore.

Forward

Benjamin M. Garrett, Sr, author: Best Seller, "Man of God"

There's a unique Scripture in the Book we call *The Holy Bible* which metaphorically contextualizes a flower to that of a female's virginity in regard to marriage. You find it in I Corinthians 7:36 as it explains the difference between an unmarried virgin and a married woman, two totally different mindsets. Yet this verse contains a phrase, *'if she is past the flower of her age...'*(KJV). This has in some areas of scholarly debate come to mean the time when a young woman has begun her cycle, an introduction of what will forever define her as woman, an internal change of her childhood self.

The Flower Girl is the embodiment of that scriptural girl in an environment which has now grown to be, in some cases, toxic ◈the Black Church. What was once a citadel of hope and a place to express one's constitutional right to religious practice has now become a cesspool of unaddressed, overlooked, and most times, ignored mental health issues. Most of these ongoing issues within the culture of churches are so psychologically trenching, they become a bigger issue of self-concealment.

We often believe that some human beings are just flat out crazy or evil, but such terms can only be an ill-assessment because we haven't included such influences in the context of poverty, drug abuse, miseducation, along with other systems of oppression. These, too, can play into criminal acts upon the victims. More importantly, such acts (within this autobiography) can force a victim to grow up too fast, circumvent people and situations and cause even extreme avoidance of true love.

Upon reading, you will come to the understanding that the words written within these pages had to have been produced from an extremely high level of vulnerability. Believing for a better world in the near future, penultimately, the first step would require one to first examine their past, no matter how dark, embarrassed, shameful, or uneasy the mental and emotional time machine would be.

It takes a courageously unique spirit to initiate an iron constitution of willful bravery, to cause one to release an autobiography that acts as a catalyst for the exposition of the ill-psychological mindset of the religious social club which we call "church" ⬦these modern-day temples, synagogues, tabernacles, or whatever nomenclature we could enumerate to exact an appeal to the religious mind. But are we yet in attendance to learn more about spirituality in depth? OR is there something utterly wrong with the communal psyche as it relates to the sociology of churches within the African American community? The content and context swirling about her is in contrast and conflict between her and the community she holds so dear, making this writing daringly unique.

Contents

THE FLOWER GIRL

Introduction

This book is based on true life events. Many names used are fictitious to protect the identity of the people who are connected or related to the abusers. The details outlined reveal how my life's journey from age 3 to adulthood was infiltrated with incest, molestation, fear, hatred, confusion, suppressed animosity, depression, identity theft and spiritual deception. But it also reveals that the love of God is a powerful weapon of mass destruction in the face of the enemy.

Throughout the darkness and hopelessness created by the enemy, the awesome power of God's love can love us beyond our situations. When we feel unloved, God's love is there to pick us up. It gives us hope when we feel hopeless and defeated and speaks of life when everything around us appears dark and dead.

My journey displays who I was and how my life went through a series of transformational processes to my becoming a woman freed from fear, delivered, made whole ⬦finally discovering my divine purpose on earth. The journey was not easy, but now I know the "why" behind the trauma and drama. Some phases I have no answer for, but it doesn't matter because what was meant to kill me turned in my favor. In fact, my whole life is a testimony to what was meant for evil God can turn it around for your good. What proved to be my hardest test became my greatest testimony.

I was inspired to write this book by *the Holy Spirit*, to help all who have struggled or now struggle with abuse, molestation, rape, fornication, adultery, low self-esteem, loneliness, timidness, sadness, hurt, pain, sickness, disease, confusion, nervous breakdown, rejection, anger, hatred, unforgiveness, promiscuity, suicide attempts, witchcraft, betrayal, guilt, drinking alcohol, drugs, lies, deceit, and secrets.

In an article, *The Ramifications of Incest*, it was stated that by the year 1986 some form of father-daughter incestuous activity – ranging from minimal to brutal and aggressive – was found in approximately 1 in 20 families, which included daughters and their natural fathers, and 1 in 7 families in which daughters resided with a stepfather. Incest often leads to traumatic bonding, a form of relatedness in which one person mistreats the other with abuse, threats, intimidation, beatings, humiliations, and harassment but also provides attention, some form of affection, and connectedness. (Richard P. Kluft, 2011)

I am breaking my silence and telling my story as a witness that these situations are happening right in our neighborhoods. Thousands of children have had the same experience as I. Some even worse. Parents and caregivers wake up and pay attention! Don't ignore the signs or cries of the children right under your nose who may need your help. These things could be happening right in your home or neighborhood to someone you love.

This book reveals how God was always in my life even when I didn't think He cared. I felt He had abandoned me and questioned why I was even born. Was I born to be abused, misused, to be unhappy and miserable? Was this my purpose? I was mad at God for a long time and full of anger and hatred towards many who contributed to my dark life. But years later, God brought me to a place of deliverance and wholeness, and

I made peace with my past. It was then that I realized Jesus Christ had been walking with me through all the seasons of my life; He was there all the time. In fact, it was Jesus who preserved my mind and didn't allow the enemy to take me out.

My prayer and sincere desire is to help people and to bring understanding to the question: "Why bad things happen to innocent people?" People do terrible things to others for reasons due to no fault of the victims they hurt. Most of the time it is beyond themselves as perpetrators; for they are operating under the influence of another spirit that didn't come from God.

My hope is that this project will help set someone free from bondage of the mind, strongholds of the heart, and generational curses that bring on struggles and tragedies in their life. Truly the mind is powerful, and the battle of life is in the mind. The invisible enemy, satan (name not capitalized because he gets no respect from me) and his imps fight us with suggested thoughts that we eat and digest in our minds.

The writing of this book was not and is not intended to hurt or offend anyone. I was inspired and mandated by Almighty God to tell the truth, shame the devil, and bring understanding, healing, and deliverance to those who are in need; souls who have suffered as I once suffered. In John 8:32 Jesus said, *"And ye shall know the truth, and the truth shall make you free."* Authoring this book is the final chapter of my deliverance in this segment of my life, and it has been liberating to say the least. God knew my end from the beginning. It is because of Him that I feel compelled, as it is now my assignment, to let people know Jesus Christ is still the only Answer. He is the Way, the Truth, and the Life. John 14:6 (KJV)

As you walk through these pages of my life, one of challenges and seeming despair, I pray that you will witness the power of God. . . that He will stand up and prevail in your life as He has in mine.

Chapter 1

Family and Wounds of Secrets

Marigold
Representing Pain

The Boogie Man

I believe I was three years old, because my younger brother wasn't even walking yet; still crawling around on the kitchen floor. Then suddenly, I remember being on my parents' bed. Mother was coming through the front door with bags in her hands. I lay alone in their bed, watching her. I do not recall what happened or why I was in my parents' bed in the first place.

Thereafter, my early childhood memories consisted of me being dragged in the middle of the night from the bed I shared with my younger sister. Our mother worked at night and didn't get off until the next morning. This happened often throughout the years. I cannot recall how many times, nor do I remember the times before my sister was born.

All my mother's children were afraid of the dark; we slept with an oil lamp. The nights I was taken from my bed to my parents' bed, my dad would slowly turn down the flame of the lantern until it faded out. I was always afraid because I knew what that meant, and I hated it! I would hold onto my sister as he pulled and dragged me to the foot of the bed and carried me to their room.

Once he had me in their room, he would lay me down on my back. I would squeeze my eyes shut so tight and kept them closed ⬥praying to disappear! I'd do anything to be ANYWHERE else but there. I could feel him raise my gown up and pull down my panties, taking only one foot out. . . and I'd squirm and wiggle as he would do this. Then as he spread my legs apart, I began to cry "No dad, no dad... Pleeease, NO!" trying to prevent what had become inevitable.

As he climbed on top of me... tears continued to roll out of the sides of my eyes, down into my ears and onto their pillow. I could feel his breath on the side of my face. . . his panting, grunting, and wreaking of reefer. He would be grinding (what I thought was) my private area. He was cunning enough NOT to push too far inside of me. After what seemed like eternity had passed... as he was about to climax, he would quickly grab the towel (already placed next to him) while he would back up off me, covering his private area. I'd hear him let out a deep exhale. He'd look at me and then plop down beside me and fall asleep.

I lay there staring at the pink ceiling, too terrified to move. . . wishing I could be rescued from *the boogie man.* Very slowly putting my one foot back into the leg of my panties, I'd ease them back up and then pull my gown down. If I felt him move, I'd pretend to be asleep. He would then gather me into his arms and carry me back to my bedroom.

During these horrific encounters, my sister never said a word, nor did she ever move a muscle as I pulled on her while being ripped from our bed. It wasn't until years later that she told me that she was so petrified, she wasn't going to move no matter how much I clawed at her skin. She said she could hear me crying as he carried me out of our bedroom and could hear me still crying while in our parents' bedroom. He would return me to our bed before dawn... as if nothing ever happened, because our mother would be coming home from work soon. I was so distraught, so scared and full of terror. With flowing tears and silent cries is how I often fell asleep.

This went on for years, not every day but throughout the years whenever he was home. He said I was never to tell, or let anyone else do this act to me, or he would kill me because he loved me. He had instilled fear in me and in my brothers and sister because he was so mean. I was never going to say anything because of fear, but my sister did eventually say something to Mom. One day we were playing outside, and she went inside and said to Mom: "My daddy came in our room last night and was messing with Joy." When she called me in and asked me, I said "No, she's telling a story." (We weren't allowed to say "lie.") In my mind I was not about to get beaten or killed by him! So, I lived with this lie and suffered in silence. Having a personality of shyness and timidness, I didn't talk a lot, which made it easy to hide a dark secret.

Dad was labeled as a *mean* person. I remember, growing up, how he always whipped the boys with a belt; it was so horrible and unmerciful. I don't recall him ever whipping me or my sisters, but he would yell and curse at us, which was degrading and showed no love. He would say mean and cruel things about people, and he never allowed me to date or even have a conversation with a boy. All of this was just cruel, mean and ridiculous in my eyes!

I also can recall Dad sitting in a chair with the Bible on his lap and a joint in his hand, yelling at us to come into the house because I was outside talking to some boys who went to school with me. My siblings were playing nearby, but now we all had to come in. I was so mad and hurt and thought: 'I will be glad when I am grown, to get away from him.' I hated my life and the town ◇to say the least! I dreamed constantly of being rescued from this hellacious life.

Teenage Crush

As a teenager, I liked boys but knew I couldn't date. In High School there was a young man I especially liked, who was a senior. (I was a sophomore.) He played in the band, and I became attracted to his skill and love for music because I was also musical. I played the organ and wrote music. Music was my life! But he never approached me, though his sister and I would spend time together. She knew I liked him, but nothing ever became of the emotion, and I let it go.

During my junior and senior years, I liked a young man who had already graduated High School. He was so handsome to me, but he never approached me in that manner. He would talk to me but never made a move toward a relationship until years later ◇after I left town and returned for a short time.

David was a Mexican boy I met at church; he was visiting from California. This young man used to visit with our pastor, and we became pen pals. He was a really good friend to me. I remember one night after church, my dad started saying some negative things about boys. . . in his loud and threatening voice. He told me that I "would never get married no matter how old I got to be! That he "didn't care if I was twenty-five." That stung me! His words hurt and stuck in my mind because of the power he had over me. He planted a seed and put it in the atmosphere. I felt hurt, defeated, and helpless.

From that point on, my dream of ever becoming a wife and mother seemed to be just that, a *dream*. That is when hate started to really manifest deep in my heart: I hated living in the house with him. I hated the church and its leadership. I always hated the city where I was born. I genuinely believe *home* is where your heart and happiness lie; but for me, my place of birth was never *home*, only the place where I lived. As far as I was concerned, there was nothing pleasant or desirable there; everything was so dismal, with nothing to look forward to. My life was as dark and depressing as it could get. I was absolutely miserable!

Devoted Wife and Mother

My mother was *saved*, a Christian woman very devoted to God and their marriage. She loved my dad, whom she thought loved her and was a saved Christian as well. I never witnessed him being affectionate or just showing love toward her as her husband. Mother was always a kind, loving and affectionate person who showed a lot of love, not only to him but to everyone. She believed in wives being submissive to their husbands, according to Scripture. Dad was the head of the house, and she reverenced him as such. She didn't make decisions without including him and/or getting his permission.

One day while they were arguing, he grabbed Mom and started to choke her. We were screaming, "Stop! Stop!" as Mom was gasping for breath. All at once, my sister grabbed a broomstick and our brother and I yelled, "Hit him!" Dillae started hitting our dad to keep him from killing our mother, or so we thought. When he realized she was hitting him, he turned toward her with *fire* in his eyes. . . you could see the evil that was upon him! We yelled for her to run, and she ran outside, running for her life! He caught her and started hitting her with hard blows. Thankfully, his brother was outside and was able to get him to get off her, to stop!

My parents' relationship was rocky and unstable to say the least; it started before I was born. The truth is, I have a sibling who is nine months younger than I (his child by another woman); two other siblings conceived with our babysitters; another sibling with a lady whom he had an affair with for years, and my youngest sibling is by one of my schoolmates.

For years I tried to understand why my mother stayed with him, after my dad was unfaithful to her most of their marriage. Over the years, the most peaceful times in our house were when my dad would leave and stay gone for an extended period. The atmosphere in our house was so different when he was away. But, after weeks or even months had passed, and without warning, he would be home when we came in from school. Mom would always let him return, again and again. The last time she let him talk his way back to coming home, we begged her not to, but she did. From her point of view, it was a hard decision since he was still her husband. This was not the first time he had talked his way back into our home and it probably wasn't going to be the last. However, four out of us five children didn't want him back home. We finally had to come to the realization that this was the fate of our household.

To us (me and my 3 younger siblings directly under me), Dad was *crazy* and *mean*: however, our baby sister loved him and could find no fault in him. But she wasn't born during the times he did a lot of the beating and raping. He favored her and spoiled her; something he had never done with the rest of us; consequently, she felt differently than we did about him. At the time, I didn't care how she felt and that made me treat her *mean* at times ◈I didn't want her to like him at all, period! But I was glad he didn't hurt her as he had the rest of us.

Musical Family

My family is exceptionally talented and gifted in singing, playing instruments, teaching music, writing music and dance. Musical gifts come from both sides of the family: my mother and her twin sister were well-known singers in the city and sang at several church events. Dad started a community choir called *The Voices of Faith.* He also played piano, guitar & saxophone but didn't make a career out of it. Consequently, my siblings and I are all very musical. We are a family of singers, musicians, composers and recording artists.

In our household we were taught to use our gifts and talents to serve in the church house. We were not allowed to listen to secular music – referred to as "the blues" – unless Dad was home. He introduced my siblings and me to a variety of songs and artists we would not have known existed. Like him, we developed a love for various musical genres: gospel, the Blues, R&B and Jazz, because our dad played them all. Later in the book, you will see how this background saved me from going crazy.

I found an escape from all the madness through music, singing, directing the choir, authoring both stories and music. But my passion was playing the organ. Being a church baby and raised Apostolic/Pentecostal gave me a great love for gospel music. Sometimes, I would go to church with my mom or grandmother to clean or sell food for the church. . . then always steal away to play the organ. I loved those times because they gave me an escape from the dreariness of my life; I could lose myself in my music. I literally spent hours playing and, in my mind, would shift into another world where there was no pain or fear.

Secret Fears

Feeling sad all the time was something I learned to live with. I would smile through my pain. My feelings were well hidden, or so I thought. But if you look at some of my pictures you can see the sadness in my eyes and in my countenance. Yes, there were some fun things I did growing up, and as a teenager, but (in my mind) no one knew the secret I was fighting so hard to conceal. Knowing this was wrong, of course, made me feel sad but it became my norm. I was trapped! Constantly living in fear of this undesirable act haunted me, especially when my mom was at work. Mom worked in the healthcare field, and I hated when her shift would change, and she would have to work nights.

Later, all this made me hate myself, and I just wanted to die. The times when I felt that this sexual act was going to happen, I would beg to stay overnight at my grandparents' house, which was a safe haven: a place of refuge, peace, joy, love, protection, and good food. My maternal grandparents' house was *the* place to be where all my siblings and cousins wanted to stay. Sometimes I wished I could live with them; I didn't want to stay home if my dad was there. We loved being at our grandparents' house, truly a loving home.

Witchcraft

At some point I was given a *Ouija* board. We thought it was just another game and wanted to see if it worked as advertised. One night my brothers, sisters, and cousins sat at the table in our kitchen where I led us in using the *Ouija* board, and it worked! We asked questions and the *Ouija* board would spell out the answer. This was amazingly scary, yet intriguing (an open door for the devil, an entry point for supernatural evil).

I later discovered that if I stared into people's eyes, I would make them scared. (Sometimes I could see things in them and tell them, not knowing I was dabbling in a world of darkness.) I would stare at some of my classmates until they started crying. And I made dolls to torture people who would bother me. Secretly, I wanted to be a "good witch" ◈always watching the sitcoms *Bewitched* and *I Dream of Jeannie,* wanting to do magic and make my life better. There is no such thing as a "good witch" and honestly, I really didn't have a heart to just hurt people. Yet at times I wanted to hurt those who hurt me. I wanted to put a spell on my dad to stop all his ungodly acts toward me, my mother, and my siblings.

Later in life, I learned that the spiritual world is real. There is the spiritual realm and the natural realm. I know now that demons (fallen angels) have been around since they were kicked out of Heaven with Lucifer, who is now the devil. They know everyone from their past who has gone on to their life's eternity. They imitate and can take on the form of our loved ones, trying to make us think the dead have been conjured up from a world beyond us. Deception! So, when there are mediums, fortune tellers, etc. that say they are in contact with the spirit of our loved ones, it's a lie from the enemy (satan). Don't believe it! Those who are saved and leave this earth are asleep. Those who are not in Christ are dead! The Bible says, "the dead know nothing" (Ecclesiastes 9:5-6 NLT) and that satan "is a liar and the father of lies" (John 8:44 NLT).

It is not good to entertain or dabble in the world of darkness; this is not the plan of God for a believer's life. We must seek God and the kingdom of Heaven only (see Matthew 6:33 KJV). Opening doors of darkness can bring much evil into your life, deceive you, and cause you to believe a lie. God is not the Author of confusion and because His Word is truth, what the Bible says about witchcraft is true, period! (See Galatians 5:19-20; Leviticus 19:26, 20:27 KJV)

Identity Theft

Growing up I felt a love/hate emotion with my dad, and it caused me to be depressed as a child. I lived in emotional overload. Dad never called me by my birth name; he gave me another name, *Suzie.* Later, I learned that Suzie was the name of a glove, commonly referred to as the *Suzy Glove. . .* mainly used by men in prison to bring themselves sexual pleasure.

I refer to this as identity theft because my dad stole my identity from me and gave me a false identity. Joy was not in my eyes or my life. Satan used him in an attempt to steal my true identity. He tried to change my purpose by inflicting fear, shame, doubt, low self-esteem, rejection, defeat, and feeling unloved. My dad used me to fulfill his own soulish, selfish, satanic desires and I suppose, if he had his way, it would have gone on indefinitely. But thanks be unto God who always causes me to triumph! I am no longer a victim; I am a victor and victorious in Christ Jesus!

My name is Joyce, but my family and others call me *Joy.* The attributes and meaning of my name had been hidden beneath this false identity. My name means joy, joyous, happiness, cheerful, merry, and "lord" [Wikipedia, Sheknows.com/baby-names/name/Joyce]. The Urban Dictionary adds radiance, a light in every person's life she touches. When she walks in a room, sometimes you can't help but stare at her because she radiates beauty and style with her presence.

Chapter Summary/Key Takeaways

When reared in an atmosphere laced with dark secrets and fear, you can grow up to be wreck. Dysfunctional homes can cause negative emotions and mindsets. But God can take what the devil meant for evil – what was intended to destroy you – and turn it around for your good and His Glory!

Chapter 2

Church, Salvation, and Safe Place

The Daisy
Representing Innocence, Beauty, Salvation & Purity

Church Background

I was born into a family of devout Christians who stood fast on the profession of their faith. They weren't "playing church." They were true born-again believers, prayer warriors whose foundation was built on the Word of God. My mom, grandma and auntie received Jesus as their Lord and Savior and were baptized in the name of our Lord Jesus, and filled with the baptism of the Holy Ghost before I was born.

Being raised in church, I was taught who Jesus is, who God is. Believing that He is all-knowing, all-powerful and every-where at the same time raised my curiosity. My question was "If God is all that, why is He allowing me - an innocent, help-less child - to be molested and plagued with fear at a young age?" It would be many years before I would get my answer. Yes, I asked God, "Why?" I am human and He knew I would ask. . . just as people today ask: "God, why did this or that happen?"

Salvation Experience

At an early age, I was taught about Jesus, His birth, death, and resurrection. However, it wasn't until I was 9 years old that I decided to get baptized. It happened on February 25, 1968, during a Sunday night service. Back in those days we literally dwelt in the house of the Lord all the days of our lives.

I believed then and still do to this day that Jesus is the Son of God, and He is God in the flesh who came to earth. He was born as a baby to a virgin named Mary. Then He died a gruesome death for my sin and the sin of all humans. They buried Him in a borrowed grave, but on the third day, He arose from the dead! ◈therefore conquering death, so that salvation would be given to all who would receive Jesus as their personal Lord and Savior.

Repenting of my sins and being baptized meant that I was making a public declaration, I was changing my life. Being buried in water signified that the old me was dead to sin; and the new me would rise to walk in a new life with Jesus. I desperately wanted a new life. So, I got baptized, but I knew there was still more to it. I needed baptism of the Holy Ghost, with the evidence of speaking in tongues as the Spirit of God gave utterance. It is a precious gift from God.

Then Peter said unto them, "Repent, and be baptized every one of you in the name of Jesus Christ for the remission of sins, and ye shall receive the gift of the Holy Ghost" (Acts 2:38 KJV).

On several occasions, during our church services, the pastor would ask if anyone wanted the Holy Ghost. Most of the time I didn't go to the altar. But my grandmother, Mama Lucy began talking about the end time, hell, fire, and brimstone to the young people. She talked about how to go to Heaven; what it meant to be saved, and how much Jesus loved us. She said you must have the Holy Ghost to be caught up in *the rapture.* I pondered her words constantly, and I wanted the Holy Ghost. I wanted to have God's Spirit living on the inside of me! I needed something that could deliver me from the horrible secret life of sin and abuse I was forced to live. Grandmom's words gave me hope for deliverance, for a better tomorrow.

When I went to church, I knew we would have what was called a *tarrying* service, which meant we were waiting on God to fill us with His Spirit, with the evidence of speaking in tongues. We would praise Him while waiting to be filled because God dwells in the midst of praise. Many times, I would *try* tarrying until I was tired, sleepy, and drained of energy. I wanted the Holy Ghost. In my head and my mind, I wanted to be filled; however, looking back I believe I could not concentrate on worshiping God, allowing Him to be the center of my attention, because of everything else that had me so weighed down.

One day I was overcome with sadness and hurt. I wanted God so badly, to talk to Him about my life. I praised and worshiped Him until He gave me the Holy Ghost. In my soft-spoken, quiet voice, I began talking to Him. The more I poured out my heart to Him, the more I could feel His presence and my voice got louder and louder. My grandmother (Mama Lucy) was my "midwife"; she kept saying, "Talk to Him and tell Him all about it." The power of God showered down on me, and praise erupted from my belly! Finally, I was in the middle aisle speaking in tongues as the Spirit of God gave me utterance. Thus, my Heavenly language was born. . . and I spoke to God as if there was no one else in the building but Him and me. Chills come even while thinking about how He baptized me and filled me with His glory. Oh, what a glorious day!

Authoring this book has caused me to have flashbacks. I can still see in my mind's eye how I walked the aisle at the church house, talking to God. So overjoyed, seeing myself before God, telling Him whatever was in my heart! No one knew my conversation with Him. This experience caused me to love God Almighty even more. Truly, Jesus is the Answer for life's problems!

Afterwards, I remember feeling so light as if I could fly. Happiness flowed over me because I now knew that I would go to Heaven if I died. The funny thing is that we were taught that we needed the Holy Ghost so we wouldn't go to hell; but

I found out it was so much more than that. Actually, it was years before I really recognized the real importance of having the Holy Spirit in my life.

After receiving the Holy Ghost that night, I wanted all my friends to have the same experience. Shortly thereafter, Faith began actively seeking the Lord for the Holy Ghost; she was inspired by my experience. Below is her point of view on its effect on her.

Faith's Viewpoint

"Joyce's grandmother had a loving relationship with the young people. She was our Sunday School teacher, choir director, altar worker, and more. Her love for us was genuine, and she wanted us to be saved. She talked to us every chance she got about salvation and would have tarrying services periodically. This particular night as we were on our knees, she was praising and praying and going around to each one of us to help us push through.

Other saints were working with us, too. I was on my knees calling on Jesus when I heard a shift in the atmosphere. The praise was getting louder, and I felt desperate for His presence in the air. Mama Lucy was saying, "Say, 'Thank You, Jesus'" and everybody was saying it with all their might so much that the power of God just came and sat in the building. There was an indescribable sound in the atmosphere and the saints started speaking in tongues and dancing *in the spirit*. It was as if a wave of God's glory came and dwelt among us.

Even without the Holy Ghost, I could feel the Presence of God all over me. When I raised up and opened my eyes it was hazy in the building; several people were lying prostrate on the floor or under a pew, some were on the altar crying out to God. But then, I saw Joyce in the middle aisle speaking in tongues, praising, and magnifying God with a loud voice. Mama Lucy was with her, telling her to tell God all about it. I stared hard because I couldn't believe it was Joyce! I wept uncontrollably because I knew I needed it more now than ever.

When I went home, I shared with my mother all the things I had witnessed. I cried some more then and every day afterwards. All the words I had heard about *the rapture* echoed in my ear and all I knew was that I had to be *saved*. I needed it like the Bible said, and as Joyce had received right before my eyes. From that night forward I begged for somebody to tarry with me, even on nights when we didn't have church. Witnessing Joyce's outpour penetrated my spirit, and I was hungry for the Holy Ghost. Thank God, He filled me too."

For the promise is unto you, and to your children, and to all that are afar off, even as many as the LORD our God shall call (Acts 2:39 KJV).

Playing the Hammond B3 Organ

My mother and auntie (who are twins) began singing at an early age in their hometown of Brownsville, TN, and were well known in the South. I played the organ for our church until I left the "King City" at age 18. Old-school organ players will understand and know what I mean when I say, "The music, the sound, and smell of the Hammond B3 organ starting up and hearing the hum of the Leslie speaker was a part of me."

Now my god sister, Esther also played the organ and piano as well. "Church people" tried to sow seeds of discord between us to the point we eventually had to go by a schedule (made by the Pastor), to play each week. Piano was not something I played well; my gift and comfort lay with the organ, but I had to comply with the schedule. It made me hurt and angry since I wasn't good at the piano like Esther; and feelings of resentment, anger, bitterness, and animosity overtook me. People will create a platform like "Showtime at the Apollo" even in the church house. That was never a stage I desired, for whenever I played, it was for God and God alone.

Even when the people were blessed, it never entered my mind that it was because of me, or about me or my playing. God used me as an instrument to play an instrument to bless His people. I stayed focused on the Father in Heaven. When I look back, I now realize that He created me to worship Him ◇for Him to receive the glory! It was all about Him.

There were times when playing the organ that I couldn't contain myself; I would lose myself in worship and go far into the Holy of Holies. People would tell me how they were blessed; that they felt *the anointing* as I ministered. One of our pastors anointed and prayed over my hands and fingers in a service and from that day forward God was in control of my playing even more. I remember playing until it felt like my fingers were playing every key. There was a sound that God enjoyed, and I enjoyed playing for Him. Sometimes, the Spirit of the Lord would come in so strong until I would get up from the organ and dance with all my might before the Lord.

At age 16 and 17, I started playing for another church and helping their choir on the Sundays I was scheduled to play the piano at my church. I was happy to get away and play somewhere other than my church house, and I really liked seeing their choir's progress. It felt as if they really appreciated me;

I appreciated them as well. This relationship lasted approx-imately a year as I was awaiting High School graduation. I couldn't wait to say goodbye to the church people, its leader-ship, and that God-forsaken city forever––or so I thought.

The Anointing, Gifts & Callings Come Without Repentance

My grandparents had always served and taken care of the pastors and their families by feeding them and accommodat-ing them with a room to sleep in on Sundays. This was a part of our lives, and we became close to their children, if they had children. The point I want to make is there was a trusted re-lationship we all developed with the pastors. Because my dad was in and out of our home, a couple of them became *father figures* to us.

I must be honest and transparent in order to help someone else who may be going through, or has been through what I'm about to reveal:

In the early 70s, our pastor became the Overseer of two churches in two different cities. He was anointed and had a great relationship with the young people. I was about 14 or 15 years old and sometimes traveled alone with him, or with others, to play for the other church. I can't remember how or when this unnatural, ungodly, unholy, adulterous relationship started. The pastor would travel to our city to be in town for Bible Study and, as always, was welcomed into our home to sleep. We were glad that someone we trusted was there at night while our mother was working overnight.

He would always sleep in our recliner chair, and at some point during the night he would engage in sexual acts with me. I recall one time when I found myself bleeding the next day and called him to ask why this happened, he said "it was natural." That's it! I never said a word about this incident, but I did not believe his was a true statement because it had never happened with my dad.

All my life when this happened, the words "I love you" were used. In my mind, the connection with those three words and sex meant the person loved me. How naive! But even though I was being taken advantage of, something inside my soul and spirit didn't feel right ◇ especially when he added that I had to keep it a secret, which was the same thing my dad always said! Being a pastor, an anointed man of God, and "holy," he must have known this wasn't right!

I must say that the mind is enormously powerful. My mind wrestled between two opinions: it was two-fold like the norm, and yet wrong, because it had to be done in secret and I was never to tell. Not talking, or talking, about sexual things became the norm for me, but inside I felt confused, alone, and really sad.

Truth

When a child's mind is influenced and trained to believe an act is normal, it becomes their norm. These sexual encounters lasted a long time in my mind, and I just wanted it to end. I was like a human machine being used to participate in an act without any understanding. Today, I believe that the fear and abuse I received from my dad caused me to become *easy prey* for pastors and other men in leadership who also took advantage of me.

There was an affiliate pastor who kissed me while the congregation was fellowshipping and engaging in hugging each other. He put his tongue in my mouth during this part of the service. He and his congregation believed in not only hugging but kissing. After that, I stopped hugging. . . withdrew myself from hugging. Still now I can envision it and reflect on how this confused me. I didn't tell anyone because my dad taught me not to tell.

A year later our pastor was removed, and the assistant pastor was chosen to be his replacement. He wasn't dismissed because of me because, to my knowledge, no one knew about his acts of molestation and adultery. It was the decision of the Presiding Bishop to remove him, which many of our church members were not happy with; nor were the young people because he was good at interacting with the younger ones. But I was relieved!

Now, the new pastor never got out of order with me, but he teased me because I was always sick, my stomach hurt all the time. I didn't like his teasing because it caused others to say that I wanted attention; they said things to indicate they thought I was a *hypochondriac.* Suffering in silence for years and having my spiritual leader initiate teasing caused me to inwardly build a wall against ever getting close to or trusting preachers. Such mistreatment caused me to become bitter, to harbor traits of hatred toward others in the body of Christ.

One time, the pain was so severe that I passed out at a school "Sock Hop" event and was rushed to the hospital. An exploratory surgical procedure was performed, and they couldn't figure out why I was sick, why I had passed out. At another time, I couldn't walk because I was so weak; however, the doctors never thought to give me a pelvic exam, rather they prescribed nerve pills. I don't know their diagnosis because it was never shared with me. I guess the doctors also thought I was a hypochondriac or maybe a teenager having mental depression.

Now, today, I know this was a part of God's divine plan, and He received the glory for the miracle that would later be revealed. My mom, grandmother and aunt prayed, and for a while I was fine. I did not just live with physical pain; my life was rife with mental and emotional pain as well. I was physically sick and full of mental anguish because of the abuse I was enduring and being forced to keep a horrible secret. It was destroying me, causing me to die a slow emotional death.

One day I was so depressed, I just wanted to go to sleep and never wake up! So, I took some pills and went out to our front porch (which was closed in with new carpet) and lay down on the floor and went to sleep, thinking I would be in Heaven and out of pain. Well, nothing happened because I'm authoring this book. I just had a good, long nap. . . suicide was no longer an option. Thank God! He didn't let it work.

So, I decided to run away and ran to a relative's house, never revealing my secret, just telling them that my dad was just too mean; and I didn't want to stay at home! They talked to me for hours and convinced me to go back home.

A Safe Place

Everyone, especially children, need and deserve a safe place to confide their secrets. It's good when parents can be that safe haven. Unfortunately, some children do not feel their parents are a safe place to go when they are upset and need to confide in someone; when they're in need of help, or even danger. How parents respond to their children determines whether they find their safe place.

There are many adults today who have trouble opening up to someone. When asked who they had to talk to as children, often they admit, they didn't feel they had anyone with whom they could share. . . and history repeats itself. When children don't feel safe to open up to their parents, or parents make no effort to be a safe place, children learn to internalize their feelings instead of sharing them in a safe, wholesome relationship. The outcome is not a good one.

Children look to their parents not only for love and support, but for protection in order to feel safe. When parents are distant and/or dealing with mental illness, substance abuse, or other issues, they are typically not able to meet the needs of their children. When a child does not have his or her emotional needs met, developmental changes occur within the brain. Changes occur at the cellular level of the brain within the hippocampus and gray area, which can result in immune and relational problems later in life. Research has shown that when a child does not have someone to connect to or their emotional needs are not being met, they will disconnect as a means of coping (Scott, 2017).

The day I found my safe place was a day when I was riding around town with Faith and her sister, Nita. I was sitting alone in the back seat; the music was playing, and we were engaging in small talk about nothing in particular. I felt really sad, depressed and alone, even though I wasn't alone. My secret was eating at my very soul, and I needed a release. I don't remember the exact song that was playing, but the music set the tone. I was literally at my breaking point; and the Lord knew it was time – and He set it up.

Nita discerned the anguish I was feeling, got out of the front seat and into the back seat with me. She held me in her arms and began praying. God used her to minister to me in a way no one else had been able to do. I knew God had revealed to her all that I was going through. She understood, without me saying a word, the pain, agony, hurt, and fear I was feeling. I wept sorely as I released this horrible secret––my first confession. Never had I confessed to anyone in my family before moving to Detroit. The release kept me from losing my mind. . . finally, I found a safe place.

Chapter 3

The Great Escape & New Beginning

Black Dahlias
Represent Betrayal, Shame & Negativity
(Hidden Is Elegance & Prosperity)

Lost in Identity Crisis

The school year was coming to an end, graduation day was approaching. It had been decided that I would go to live with my aunt and uncle in Detroit. One of the happiest days of my life was soon to come! Each day we would sneak some of my clothes to my grandparents' house to pack for the long-awaited escape. (My cousin/brother William was going to accompany me to Detroit and stay for a couple of weeks.) The wait seemed long, but anticipation made me feel good just knowing I wouldn't have to continue living in fear and unhappiness. In my mind, anything would be an improvement.

Graduation came and went. The next week would be my departure from a town I hated because of all the pain I suffered. My clothes were all packed and secure at my grandparents' house. Bible Study was typically on Wednesdays. That Wednesday night, June 30, 1976, after service, we loaded the car, and I said goodbyes to my family, with the exception of my dad. We were off to Detroit! Relief and freedom from bondage swept over me when we reached the outskirts of the small town. My god sister (referred to as Faith) was my best friend, who along with my other god sister, Esther, knew of my unhappiness and my abusive dad. However, Esther did not know my secrets.

Faith and her mom helped me to escape my hellish life by driving my cousin and me to Indiana. I never referred to the town as my home because my heart was never there, and I felt the town caused me unhappiness, pain and suffering. For years I dreamed of my escape, of living in the city of Detroit with Auntie and Uncle. Finally, that prayer was answered.

Cousin William and I took the bus from Indianapolis where our ride ended in Detroit; this was going to be my new home.

We arrived in the *Motor City,* and I got settled in my new home, with a sigh of relief. I was happy! I was free! The first couple of weeks my aunt showed us around the city, connecting us with family members I hadn't seen for a few years. My big cousin Ruby and I were always close. She was my "big sister," and we spent a lot of time together, talking all the time. She discerned that I came to Detroit not only to go to school, but that there was something deeper. I confessed nothing other than that I always loved Detroit and had wanted to live there since I was a young girl. Ruby didn't force the issue, but I knew she didn't believe that was my main reason for moving to Detroit.

New Beginning

My former pastor, Elder Harold had suggested a church which I visited and later joined. The Greater Grace was where Aunt Lottie also attended. It was a mega church, and they had many musicians, so I never found a place as a musician there. One of the pastor's daughters, Star, and I became close friends. We spent time together a lot, usually at their home, where I became well acquainted with the family. But soon I drifted away because I was not engaged or connected in ministry; I felt confused and lost. Everyone needs a nail in the church. Back home I played the organ, sang, and directed the choir. Now at this new church, I was inactive with no real ministry connection. All the hurt and painful memories of my past began to flood my mind; it wasn't long before I started to think that "church" was not the answer for me.

Back home I learned how to put on a false face in public. I covered up my pain by being active in the church and filling my schedule with busyness, thus avoiding the root cause of my dilemma. I felt no one in the church cared. I was afraid, so why would I tell them my story? They only cared about doing things in the church; dancing and praising God, which is good ◇ for God always deserves our praise, no matter what our circumstances are!

But it felt that the church was deceived about the true state of the people all around them; and what was worse, it felt as if they didn't care. They weren't concerned about reaching those people with deep-seated problems, pain and hurt. If this was not the case, then where was their discernment for those needing healing, deliverance, and to be made whole not just spiritually, but emotionally. Sometimes I felt like shouting, "Wake up!"

I always wondered why no one could see that I was hurting and in pain. God gives you Holy Ghost power and discernment is what I was taught, but no one could discern or *see* in the *spirit* what was being done to me or *look into my soul* through my sad eyes. I would always ask God: *Why so much pain? So much sadness?* and *Lord, why me?* I didn't understand. One of my favorite songs I always requested Esther to sing was "I Must Tell Jesus"; it gave me temporary relief. I just wanted to be happy, wanted to feel the joy we were taught, that which we sang about. *Where was God? Where was Jesus in my life?*

I wanted to just end it and go to sleep forever. The tears I cried, the bad dreams, nightmares, and emptiness I felt was sometimes unbearable. At that point, my bad days always out-weighed my good days, because I could barely recall the good days. The times when I was happy, or at least bearable, were when I could lose myself playing the organ. Later, I learned to escape my emotions through listening to music and dancing.

The Guys Next Door

There were two handsome guys next door, and one was the most handsome guy I had ever seen. Something about him tugged at my heart! I asked my aunt about him, and she said, "Girl, every girl on the block has tried to get with him. But let me tell you how to get his attention." I laughed, but I listened. He would watch me walking to the store with my little cousins. I would always speak and keep going, never stopping to have a conversation. I was the new girl on the block, somebody different. . . there's something about "church girls" that seems to draw attention. I had never dated or had a boyfriend, so this was new to me. Ironically, Kimbell had the same kind of car and same color as Uncle Lonnie. Whenever I saw the car coming down the street, I would get butterflies in my stomach: was it him or my uncle?

One evening my little cousin Kev and I were sitting on the porch, and Kimbell came outside and started walking toward us. Excitement arose and I felt a fluttering in my stomach as he was coming up the sidewalk. *Wonder what he wants? Why was he coming over?* He walked up and introduced himself. I told him my name and we started talking. That day we talked a long time, mainly small talk, just getting to know each other. Later that week, he asked if he could take me for a ride and I said, "Yes." It was a beautiful night and he drove me to Belle Isle Park. With the moonroof open and the nice breeze coming through, I felt relaxed and comfortable. We parked, talked, and talked for what seemed to be hours.

While listening to Norman Connors' song, "You Are My Starship," he leaned over and kissed me. OMG! (Oh my gosh!) This was my first kiss from a man I actually liked, and I welcomed it. It was indescribable and unimaginable; the softest, sweetest, and most loving kiss I had ever experienced. To this moment in time while reminiscing, I can still feel the effects of that kiss. We talked more and drove from the park continuing to talk while holding hands until we arrived at our homes. It was quite convenient to walk me to my door, give me a good night kiss and then walk next door to his home. Oh, what a night! A night I will always remember and cherish.

From that day forward we began spending a lot of time together. He rocked my world, and I was full of newfound joy! After a few weeks, my aunt noticed I was not eating much. It was as if I had forgotten to eat. I told her I did not have an appetite. Auntie said, "Girl, you are *in* love!" This man made me happy, which was something I never experienced nor was I used to, and I fell *in* love with him. He listened to me with his heart and talked to me about my problems, hurt and pain. He never tried to force me to have sex. When he finally asked, I told him I was not ready, and he was so understanding and patient it was unbelievable. He was with me because of me and not my body. Of course, he liked my body, but he also enjoyed just being with me. He always said I was so sweet. At this point I didn't know if he loved me or was just in "strong like"; but we had a beautiful relationship and we were close friends.

Side Note: I was raised wearing dresses or skirts all of the time, so I didn't own any slacks or shorts. One Sunday afternoon we were going to Belle Isle Park when Auntie said, "You can't go hang out in the park in a dress or skirt!" So, she got me some jeans, which felt so weird at first, but were wonderfully comfortable. We hung out there and I had the best time I had ever had, other than being at a church service. I felt so free and liberated to run, jump, and play ball without restrictions. *Truth Revelation:* To my surprise, I found out that pants won't send you to hell. Clothes have nothing to do with our salvation or relationship with Almighty God. Again, the bondage of religion! This new freedom was amazing, and Auntie took me shopping! I thought *Hmmmm, watch out Kimbell; I'm about to be really cute.*

My Emotional Release

One night I was at Ruby's house; she was having a little party. She introduced me to some of her friends and I somewhat interacted with them yet kept mostly to myself. As the party went on, she and I went to her room to talk because - without warning - depression descended upon me. As I began to talk, I had a breakdown and told her everything. I could no longer hold my emotions about my dad and my childhood life, the reason why I moved to Detroit. I had never ever confessed anything to my family until that night when I broke down. Ruby called her dad, and he called my mom to let her know all that had happened to me. I was eighteen and having an emotional breakdown! This was not and is not a feeling I want anyone to experience. I had no control of my mind or emotions; my mental state was not stable, and I needed help! I cried and cried my eyes out (so to speak) before finally falling asleep.

After agreeing to get counseling, I remember being asked to put together puzzle pieces; stuff I had seen in movies when characters had lost their minds or had a mental breakdown. The doctors asked so many questions; some things, because of the pain and fear, I had blocked from my mind. I blocked out horrible events that happened, and I now believe my mind was being protected so I wouldn't lose it! A prescription for Valium 10mg with an unlimited refill was given to me. This pill was for nerves and anxiety, and I only took one when I felt I needed to relax.

One day, I received a call from a former Pastor EdWord who had moved to California, and he asked me to be the organist in his church. I was immediately taken back by his request, being that he also was a "BOOGIE MAN" in my life!

Yeah, so let me take you on a dreadful ride... I once traveled with him on the Greyhound bus. I went to St. Louis many times to play the organ for him at the other church. One night on the way back home he whispered, "let's go to the back of the bus." So, me being the obedient, passive, and naïve girl I was... I followed him.

It was around 2am, so not many people were on the bus. When we got back there, he told me to have a seat. I sat down, he sat beside me, and began to rub my leg. Of course, I felt very uncomfortable with him doing this to me. As he was touching me, he said "it's alright, I'm not gonna hurt you, I love you Joyce. Being that this has happened so much in my past, I had become numb to it and began to think IS it wrong or is it okay?

With the hour being so late, I was dozing off and was awoken by him kissing me on the lips and his hands were inside of my panties. He grabbed my waist and pulled me up on top of him. A thought ran across my mind, "you just preached and preached GOOD! What are you doing?" I know this is definitely wrong. Yet I had become immune to this dysfunctional behavior, with a distorted perception of reality I felt they loved me, and this is how it was shown.

He dozed off after he had his way with me. I remember staring out of the window trying not to let him or anyone else hear me crying. We entered MTV, got to the bus station and grabbed a cab to my house. When I arrived home, my mother greeted us... YES, I said us!! He was so trusted by my mother and most all the other church members. He was welcome to spend the night when he didn't want to drive home over the highway, or he had meetings in town the next morning. As I walked to my bedroom, he sat in the orange recliner in our living room and fell asleep as if nothing had ever happened.

Okay, back to my California invitation. I had never been to California, so I decided, after I graduated from technical school, to work and make some money to go there to play at his church. Traveling by bus, Pastor EdWord paid for the ticket, and it took me about three days, but it was an enjoyable ride, stopping in different states along the way. I remember when I arrived, I stayed with Pastor EdWord and his family for a couple of weeks before moving in with a friend I met from the church. He never approached me in a sexual way.

I played the organ for the church, but it was not the same; I wasn't playing for Almighty God, I was just playing. Even though I loved playing the organ, I lost my passion because I focused more on my past. One afternoon Pastor EdWord wanted to speak to me. He said he knew about my dad and what he had done to me. I was speechless and completely shocked!! Although the encounters the pastor had with me happened a few years prior to me going to California. I couldn't help but wonder... Instead of trying to help me, he took advantage of me and did the same thing my father did!! What type of sick man was he?! I now wanted to go back to Detroit.

While living in California, my friend David and I were still close, and his mother became one of my godmothers. I stayed at their home pretty often. Depression came over me once again and she was so comforting and attentive. I was so appreciative to her for just listening to me and being there for me. I never revealed the pastor's name to her or anyone else.

From time to time, I would take Valium to relax, so I could rest. I told Pastor EdWord I could no longer play for the church or live in California. I left California with my pastor and wife from Detroit. They happened to be in L.A. for a conference. I had called Star and she connected us so that I could come back home. After a few years had passed, I was somehow blocked Pastor EdWord and the events out of my mind. Out of sight, out of mind!

This was not a good place to be when dealing with trauma or living in denial, thinking it will pass if you block it out. Triggers store away in your subconscious waiting for their time of release. When triggered, they can cause adverse reactions, and no one knows or understands why you are reacting or behaving in such a manner. No one should ever ignore the trauma in their lives. Admitting and facing the events that took place needs to be dealt with immediately. You must have a person or confidant to talk to about life's problems. Freedom comes after communicating and dealing with the past and present in order to have a successful and fulfilled future.

Continual Physical and Emotional Pain

One night I was in great pain. My stomach hurt so bad I was in tears. My Tee Tee (Auntie) heard me moaning, groaning, crying out, and she rushed me to the Henry Ford Hospital. After checking me in, the nurse took me back and because I was 18, they wouldn't let my Auntie come back with me. This was a terrifying experience. As I was lying on the table, they asked me questions and I was still crying from the pain and being scared. They proceeded to examine me by pushing my stomach while I was crying profusely. They mentioned doing a pelvic exam; and I had no idea what that meant because I had never had one.

The doctor and a nurse came back with the tools and said to me, "Open your legs." *"WHAT!"* I said. So, they began to tell me what the procedure was, and when I said "No" they called for backup. They held me down to do the exam while I was screaming and asking for my aunt. I gave up fighting and they did what was necessary to examine me. This was a horrifying experience! When the results came back, they said "Young lady, you have *gonorrhea*, and it appears you have had this for several years." I asked what *gonorrhea* was, and they looked as if I should know. The doctor explained and said they would need to give me two shots in my back. The needles were so long, and to this day, I can remember how it felt going in my back. They gave me medication and instructions along with advice to see a specialist.

Now that my secret was out, the question was who gave it to me? Since no one knew about Pastor EdWord, it was blamed on my dad. I only had only been raped by two people and only Pastor EdWord penetrated; however, touching without penetration from an infected partner is a way of contracting *gonorrhea*. See (https://onlinedoctor.superdrug.com/how-do-you-catch-gonorrhea.html). Then, which man gave me the disease was a mystery.

In going through all the medication and treatment, I began getting depressed. Although many medications have side effects that include depression, mine had been ongoing off and on for years. Again, I asked, *"God, why me?"* At 18, about to turn 19 years old, I had battled with bouts of depression for a while.

The Party Life

I began working at the IRS Data Center, and I really liked my job and met a lot of people. I had one friend, Coco, who was older than me and was an awesome dancer. Coco and I would hang out with my friends, Debra and Mellow Mike (a DJ in his spare time). We would party, party, and party some more! Dancing and music became my escape – my world – and when I danced, I would move my body to the beat of every musical instrument in a song. I was in my own little world then, and I was so happy. My Tee Tee would say I danced in my sleep!

Mike taught me to DJ: I would spin records in the after-hours private D.O.T. Club and became known as *Lady J* or *Lady JJ*. I enjoyed myself tremendously. I had so much fun and was happy, but I took it too far◇ became too wild! I had started drinking, smoking cigarettes and weed/marijuana occasionally. At first it was just to be sociable, and then it turned ugly. Later, drinking and getting high for me became a means to deal with my past.

I would drink more even though I danced the night and day away; liquor was taking its toll on me. I just wanted to forget all the bad stuff, but I couldn't. My friends and I loved to party, bar hop and go to cabarets every weekend. We would always end up at the D.O.T. Club and finish about 6am with breakfast. We still went to work and did a good job.

After Kimbell left and moved out-of-state, I dated here and there, and a couple of young men were really nice. One was a city bus driver whom I liked. I tried having a sexual relationship with him after about 3 months but freaked out even when he was confessing his feelings. (I believe it was because he had the same name as my dad.) I later explained, and he wanted to continue seeing me but mentally I was not able.

It was hard to date knowing that sooner or later the man would want to have an intimate and sexual relationship. I was later told the way I danced seemed to be sexual and was very provocative. Men, relatives, and friends said it was too sexy and could send the wrong signal, which was not my goal. In my mind, this was just what I loved to do. I just wanted to dance! Dancing was fun, it made me happy. I felt free and I was a good dancer, period! Dancing freed my mind from all the negative thoughts and memories of the past. Pole and topless dancing were offered as a job, and I declined. That was not what I desired to do with my dancing gift.

One night while sleeping, Juana called me on the phone. Juana was my cousin Ruby's sister-in-law. "Wake up, I'm coming to get you," she said. "There is a dance contest and I know you will win!" I said "Really. Okay, I'll do it." Juana arrived to pick me up and when we entered this club it was packed. And the group called *The Dramatics* was about to come on stage to perform. Juana introduced me to the group's road manager; his name was Tony and he happened to be her friend. He got my name, and I entered the contest they were having shortly. All who entered had to dance to the song, "Shake It Well" (from the 1977 album *Shake It Well*). My turn came and I danced. . . had to dance with "Squirrel," a member of the group and he sang a lead part on this song. Needless to say, I was the winner.

That very week I went on tour with them, touring cities on the east coast and in the South. I had a ball! But being in a somewhat celebrity lifestyle is tiring; and it can go to your head if you're not around people who are stable and have good principles. "Squirrel" was like a big brother, and he watched after me. I believe he was the *angel* God had in my life while in the celebrity world. I became friends with the group members and a couple of the band members. They had my back because I was young and naïve, a "church girl" which many of them could tell. I truly am grateful to them for protecting me and not taking advantage of me.

More Pain

On occasion, I still suffered pain in my pelvic area. I went to see a specialist and was told I needed surgery; and there was a possibility I would need a hysterectomy. The doctor said because I was so young, he would avoid it if possible. I was put on I.V. antibiotics to help clear the infection. One tube cleared but the other had deteriorated from the disease that I had for so many years. I was so devastated, sad, confused, and angry! I cried but still had to move forward with the surgery.

When it was all over and I was awake, my Auntie and the doctor were there. He informed me that he took one tube and left both ovaries; however, the tube he left was damaged and had no filters to hold an egg. He stated he was sorry, but I would never have children. That broke my heart to say the least, and I cried and cried. This was a dream of mine, to go to college, get married and have about six children: three girls and three boys. Now I will never have even one! *Really God, why? Why me? What did I do?*

Now I'm mad at God along with my rapists, the childhood pastor who teased me for being in pain and the church people who hurt me. I didn't want to live. *For what?* Those were thoughts running through my mind. Cousin Ruby and my Tee Tee talked to me, and I understood what they were saying, but my mind wouldn't let me pass my past and the current hurts and pain. I felt sorry for myself. I pleaded and prayed to God to help me but couldn't even sense He was near. Although I was mad, I knew Almighty God from my experiences with the Holy Spirit and I still prayed.

Once I started to heal and was able to dance, I gradually did small dance movements. I started singing background with a different group that I met through a friend while in the hospital. My drinking increased, or should I say when I drank it was in excess, though not all the time. I would get high smoking weed, i.e., reefer, marijuana, whichever term you want to use. I snorted cocaine and even slept with a married man (which I hated doing because I knew what that did to my mother when her husband cheated on her). It was wrong, against my morals and beliefs, but the power of the enemy making suggestions to my mind and the results from drinking alcohol altered my thinking, and I found myself in the sheets with this man.

My friend's brother-in-law lied to me about his wife, saying she was sick, and they weren't going to be together much longer; and being young, vulnerable, naïve, hardheaded, I wouldn't listen to my cousins JL or Saul who said to stay away from him and leave him alone. This man is trouble and still married. This man supposedly loved me and was not going to be with his wife. Lies the devil will tell, lies we believe! It soon ended and I felt so bad and wanted to apologize to his wife and her sister who was my friend, but I never got the opportunity. I believe he thought I could get him and his group a break because of the people I knew in the music industry. I left the city for a while and never had any contact with any of them again. That was the first and last time I ever had an affair with a married man. To this day, I shun the very appearance and will set a married man straight who approaches me with that intention.

Detroit Exit

While enjoying the life of partying, it had to come to a halt. I honestly enjoyed party life and will say today "Sin is fun, but not all the time." Enjoying things in the flesh is something I had never experienced while growing up. There is a difference between living for Jesus - obeying the God of Abraham, Isaac and Jacob - and living a sinful lifestyle. And I was learning the difference. I did not have fun in "church" like I had fun in the streets. Religion had me bound and so did sin. In my mind I knew right from wrong, and I knew the biblical way of living which conflicted with the way I had chosen to start living. Soon I discovered that sin led to more sinful acts even if I didn't want it. There were spiritual strongholds of the mind, will and emotions; they were like "shackles" of the mind, locked up and keeping me from my divine purpose, the reason for me being born. I felt it didn't matter that I was born because of the pain in my life.

When I had a sexual encounter with my friend's brother-in-law, I knew it was wrong. I was young, and he was a manipulating older adult who took advantage of me; he had me believe that his wife was so sick, and it was okay. Now thinking back, "How could I be so gullible? That was so stupid!" And I beat myself up! I understand now how the devil tricked me and used sex and the words "I love you" as relatable. That man belonged to someone, and I was just fooled by his smooth talk and affection. It was wrong and I did it twice even though I felt bad. In fact, I had to get high to do it. It was as if I was a robot in action and I didn't even enjoy it. Wow!

The brother of the sisters liked me as a person and one night when leaving a singing rehearsal, the adulterous man volunteered to take me home, but *their brother* interrupted, insisting he would take me home. The way he looked at me and insisted, I got in his car. He told me his sisters had found out and were going to confront and attack me, and he wanted me to go to another relative's house until it died down.

I remember the unction to just leave and go back to Illinois for a while. This frightened me and, at the same time, I felt so bad for betraying the wife. From that day forward I vowed never, ever to do that to anyone else. And I never did. Any of us can make mistakes so we must think before judging some-one's actions or behavior. I left God but He never left me. And He made a way of escape when the friend and her sister found out.

While I was away, I wanted so badly to call and apologize but felt it would not be accepted. I spoke to the brother and thanked him because I knew God used him to help me escape the awaiting danger. I was able to leave and completely sever that relationship. It also allowed me to recognize all the trouble and hurt I had caused. Growing up with infidelity in my home and in the "church," I never ever should have committed this indiscretion because it hurts people, and I hate causing hurt to others.

I know firsthand what it feels like to feel hurt to the point of suicide and/or rage. The guilt of this one incident has been with me for years. I asked God to forgive me and prayed that she and her sister would somehow do the same. Many days and nights, I've cried because of this incident and believed that God would let them know I was young, naïve, and did stupid things which I truly regret. My problem was not forgiving myself; I didn't know how. If God forgave me, why couldn't I forgive myself?

Over time, the Lord walked me through the steps of self-forgiveness, and I finally forgave myself. Now, I have peace even though thoughts about what I did come to mind. However, drafting this book has been very instrumental in helping to complete my deliverance from hidden feelings and emotions that had not yet surfaced.

I want to be free of guilt and shameful deeds; free to live the rest of my life knowing I'm forgiven ⬦made free through Christ Jesus, the Head of my life. I want to live my best life and when things from the past come to mind, I will remember without guilt and shame. I did what I did. I hurt people, I'm sorry and I am forgiven for those mistakes. No longer will I entertain guilt and shame, because Jesus died so that I may be free from all sin, past, present, and future.

Chapter 4

Another beginning

Daffodils, Lilies & White Roses
Represent New Beginning

Return to Illinois

I returned to Illinois and stayed a few months in the small city I never wanted to return to from the day I left. Yes, I went back but only temporarily. I got a temporary job and moved into an apartment with my sister and her son. We lived there for about 4 months, before moving into a house near our grandparents. I dated the man that I had a crush on in High School, but it never went beyond just a physical relationship. I wanted more; I wanted him to love me as a woman, not just a sex partner.

What I thought the relationship would be was romance and love, but it was nothing but a sexual one, leaving me feeling incomplete. I yearned for true love, marriage, and family. This hurt because my dream was to be a wife and to have children, not be someone's sex partner and childless. Having children was not realistic for me but being a wife was possible. This was not what he wanted, so I stepped back out of the relationship. At this point, it was over.

I know now that sex is not love, but it was all I knew because of the words "I love you" whispered to me in the night as a young girl. I didn't like it. Getting high and drinking made it easy to have sex with the man of my teenage dreams (so I thought), but that faded away . . . I no longer had a desire to be with him.

The same place my dad worked is where I also worked for years. I got hurt on the job and lost the use of my right arm when it got caught in a dysfunctional Hyster forklift. My dad still lived in MTV, still working for that company, and happened to be there the day I was hurt. He came to see how

I was doing because I was screaming, having reverted back into a childlike state and calling "Daddy!" to help me!

I thought my arm had fallen off; and I was going into shock. The engineer had to cut the machine in half to release my arm, and after being freed, I was taken by ambulance to the hospital. My memory is vague, but I remember having a sling and being on medication. To this day I have a scar on my arm.

It appeared to me that my dad had no recollection of what kind of dad he had been. We never really talked during my short stay except the day of my accident. After I moved in 1979, he eventually moved first to Canada and then to California. This was around 1980. I never heard from him again until the year 2000.

Springfield

Living in MTV for that long was not my plan, but I didn't know where I wanted to move after leaving Detroit. I would always talk to Verne (another godmother), who truly listened to me and gave me advice about my life's situations. Our talks always made me feel better and gave me a lift after being in a state of depression. I shared with her about being the victim of incest and abuse; and talked in depth about not being able to have children. I told her about trying to decide where to move next because I hated living in MTV.

A friend, Cherlynn, suggested that I move to California with her family. I thought about it but since I had already lived there, I had no desire to go back. Verne suggested I move to Springfield; and I could stay with her and her family until I got on my feet. It didn't take long for me to say "Okay." I felt a relief that I was finally leaving again a place that had nothing to offer, a place that didn't feel like my home. It never felt like *home*.

Nothing was really accomplished in MTV after leaving Detroit. I found out that Eugene was not the man I imagined him to be and that he was not my destined husband. For my dad I still felt a love/hate relation: guess the little girl inside of me wanted him to be the father God intended him to be. I wanted to see if he would apologize for what he had done, even things he hadn't done, to make my life hell on earth. I yearned for him to show me love, naturally, like a real daddy without all the unnatural affection.

On the other hand, I hated him because he abused me, stole my identity, my innocence and left me broken-hearted, confused, and distraught. I wanted the father that I saw represented in other families, and what I saw on TV. I felt bad inside! Depression always knocked at my door and my emotions always opened the door to those thoughts, visions, and whispers I heard in my mind's ear.

In April, I moved to Springfield after staying 7 months at MTV, and there was a feeling of relief, of another new beginning, that came with that move. I started a job with Illinois Bell Telephone Company and worked a few months before accepting a job with the State of Illinois, Secretary of State division. Now, I was doing what I studied and was certified to do as a Keypunch/Data Entry Operator. I love technology and doing a job one likes gives you a feeling of happiness, but still I had emotional challenges ◈ day and nightmares thinking my dad was looking for me. This was so crazy!

Springfield was not as far as Detroit, so my mind played tricks on me. I would get depressed thinking because I had told the secret, he was going to get me. The mind is *the battlefield* where satan and his demons make suggestions to cause us to act and think a certain way. Satan can only suggest thoughts and cause us to react, he cannot make us do anything. The decision is all up to us; I never say the devil made me do anything! I repeat, the devil and his imps can only suggest thoughts to the mind and it's up to us to react.

Be aware, the power of suggestion is strong. For every suggestive thought from the Holy Spirit there is a counter thought from the evil one. When we act upon evil thoughts, we must suffer consequences from that decision. I've learned through experience that making the wrong decision will cost you. . . and making the right decision will cause a good outcome even if we don't see it in the beginning.

I didn't realize I had been in the same city with my dad for 7 months and not once did he bother me. It was after I left from there that I started having emotional trauma attacks in my mind. So, I began taking a drink here and there to calm my mind. I added Cognacs to my liquor list and then beer. I would smoke marijuana, usually with friends, which was indicative of the crowd I spent time with. Not that the crowd was bad, because they all have great jobs. All this was a temporary fix and put a Band-Aid on the wounds of my past. Partying and dancing were still a big part of my life. Soon I moved in with my sister's mom and two other sisters.

While working at *Secretary of State*, I met a handsome man by the name of Stu. We started dating but he was not one for a long-term relationship; we dated approximately 6 months. He was nice, handsome, hardworking but just not for me. One night, after partying, I was high and a little drunk, and he wanted to get freaky. I just was not the one for that kind of freaky sex. No and blank!!! No! That space is for expelling, not receiving! I broke it off.

Once again, I felt I was a magnet for sex: everyone I met wanted my body, wanted to have sex. I danced provocatively and I knew men liked it. But as I said previously, in my mind, it was entertainment and a way to express my emotions because I loved that I could express myself by moving to every instrument I heard in the music. It's hard to explain what I felt. But my mind was into the music more than into what people thought unless I was competing in a dance contest. I was *a dancing machine*, but I had not performed since leaving Detroit.

I went on dates but nothing serious developed for a while. I had fun just going out partying, just being free. One night, feeling depressed, I went to a local bar to play pool and have some drinks. I met a man who started talking to me and saw that I was distraught; he felt sorry for me. He told me his name, Wilby, but it didn't dawn on me who he was until sometime later. He was a genuinely nice and caring person. I talked with him for a few days and liked how he seemed to care about me and my issues. It was an illusional trap that I fell into; allowing the devil to suggest that this relationship was okay. He was not even my type, totally opposite of what I was attracted to or dated.

This man had been with a close relative and conceived a child as a teenager. It wasn't a serious love relationship; they were messing around satisfying a sexual urge, and a child was conceived. Although the relative and I discussed the situation in detail and both of us agreed it was okay, I knew it wasn't okay. It wasn't okay in my mind. To me it wasn't morally right. Yes, it happened, and again, we do things in life that are crazy and wrong. It even happened in the Bible. I'm not the first nor the last. Don't judge me or anyone else; for we learn from relationships and experiences. Thinking about it now I say, "Wow, how my thinking and reasoning was so off point!"

My relative was actually glad I was the girlfriend; she knew their child would be taken care of with love. One of the good things that came out of that relationship is that I established and gained some lifetime friendships. Yes, I still have those friendships today.

The man and I stayed together for four years; however, two of the years we were just roommates because he was not faithful and gave me *chlamydia.* I caught him messing around on many occasions. He apologized and tried to reconcile, but I was done; no way on earth would I ever continue an intimate relationship. I stayed in the same house, sleeping on the couch, until moving into my own apartment. It was over!

While we were in the relationship we played and sang in bands together. He played keyboard and so did I. He introduced me to three lady friends who sang previously with him. Ironically, we became close friends, and our singing group was known as WPBM (Whiteside, Pittman, Brewer & Moore). We sang in several Illinois area events, and I did our group's choreography. We are still friends to this day. Pittman has since passed.

Singing in the group was my spiritual connection, for it reminded me of church and took me back to my roots. Church was their roots as well. We would occasionally sing in churches and that felt good and natural; however, it was not enough for me to attend any church house regularly.

One memory I won't forget is being raped by one of Wilby's friends. One night we were all out at a bar called *the Metro*, which my adopted dad owned. I got drunk and told my man, Wilby, to take me home. He wanted to continue to stay out and socialize so he dropped me off and went back to *the Metro*. I went to bed because I was cramping and had started my menstrual cycle. I was awakened with this man on top of me and I recall him saying something, but it wasn't my man's voice! I hit the light and saw it was his friend McCoy, whom I didn't care for anyway. Most people didn't care for him; he had a bad reputation among many of our friends. He was tolerated because of Wilby.

The light exposed him and the blood all over his white outfit. I screamed and cussed at him as he ran out. I was crying and got to the telephone and called my adopted dad, Walter, at *the Metro*. I told him what happened and immediately he and his girlfriend Rosy came to the house, called the police and we went to the hospital. I was examined and the nurse used a rape kit. I was fit to be tied. Wilby and other friends went out looking for McCoy. The results revealed his DNA and McCoy was arrested.

All kinds of memories started resurfacing and great pain and depression overshadowed my life. Wilby was not much help because his friend, McCoy had been calling him. Wilby's mom liked McCoy a lot and she was in his ear asking him if it really happened, sowing seeds of doubt. McCoy's girlfriend, Netta, came to see me and wanted me to drop the charges, but I refused. I spoke with the DA often and we went over the incident many times and my story remained the same each time. He explained, even though it happened, and I was telling the truth, the Prosecutor was going to try and discredit my claim and bring up my past. He wasn't sure I could handle it.

Honestly, I don't think I would have made it through without having a mental breakdown.

The final straw in my decision to pursue or drop the charges happened one day when Wilby came home after being with his mother and began badgering me, asking "Did it really happened?" Immediately, I started screaming and crying and replied, "Yes! Do you mean you don't believe me, even with all the evidence? You know I never liked McCoy, and you still believe McCoy?" When he answered "Yes," my mind went into utter turmoil, torn between sanity and insanity! I started screaming and felt my mind fighting to stay sane or just give up and blank out.

Immediately something snapped within me, and my mind came back to the room. I cussed him out and went to the drawer to get my gun. I was going to shoot him! But thankfully... it was gone! Miraculously, I calmed down enough to get in my car and leave. Later, I told the DA I was not fit to go to trial, and I dropped the charges. I moved out and got my own apartment. I learned firsthand that there is a thin line between sanity and insanity. I believe in my heart God had someone praying for me at that particular time and that's why I didn't lose my mind.

Strangely, all my friends, whom I met through Wilby, believed me and were on my side. We remained close friends and, as mentioned before, we are still good friends, like family. Some of them wanted to get together and beat up McCoy, but I talked them out of it. They were hard working men with good jobs and families. One friend even devised a plan to shoot him but didn't go through with it. He said you are my sister and that #@%% needs to be shot! I talked him out of it and told him McCoy wasn't worth it. He had his own family to think about. I appreciated my brother/friend Taine and Butch for their loyalty, love, brotherhood, and friendship. Wilby claimed I took all his friends, but they were meant to be a part of my life from the start. He was just the conduit for our connection.

Before moving into my new apartment – which was a great accomplishment – I had transferred jobs from IL Secretary of State to Dept of Public Aid and then to the IL Dept. of Revenue! There I met a man whom I thought was cute. He was popular with the ladies, but I only wanted to use him for a sexual encounter. Now this relationship I wanted. He was the lead worker in my department during the tax season.

My friend and I produced more than our quota every day and were recognized for our production by him and the supervisor. I told her, "I am going to get him (Lol). Watch my moves, girl!" Every day I dressed sharply and did as my aunt had taught me when I was in Detroit. In less than two weeks, he asked me to walk and talk with him during breaks, and to have our lunch together. This was the start of a 17-year relationship. I had only wanted one night, but we became friends and lovers after the first date.

Theo and I spent a lot of time together. His friends came to know me, and they became my friends, too. (One, Alvin, was like a brother; my "ride or die buddy" until the day he passed.) Theo was a motorcycle rider and belonged to a motorcycle club. He frequented the spot where the members and guests socialized, had barbecue outings, partied, and watched sport games. I was not suffering as much from depression or nightmares; for Theo and I spent so much time together at work and after work, which occupied my mind and helped me not to reminisce so much on the past. We worked together in the same building and the same department for many years. He became my supervisor at one point, which is when I learned to separate work from our personal relationship. Most people cannot do this, but I was determined to try. . . . It was not easy.

There were times we were on the outs with each other, and I was so upset with him I would go in the bathroom and find myself crying. My buddy, Cindra, would talk to me and help me get past the hurt of the situation, and then I would act as if he were another co-worker and continue about my day. I realize, I was good at hiding pain because it was what I grew up doing. It takes strength and determination to work with someone you are dating.

It wasn't long before I started having pain in my pelvic area again. I had been told previously by my physician that having a hysterectomy was not recommended because of my age. Unfortunately, after extensive testing and lots of treatments, it was determined I was sterile and would never have children. However, on this particular visit the doctor said he would perform surgery to clean up adhesions and scar tissue. This surgery would not cause me to have hope for children but would relieve the pain I was experiencing. Theo was by my side along with friends Jean and Butch, who had always been loyal and devoted. When the surgery was over the doctor told Theo and I that the surgery went well, but I would still be unable to conceive children, which was never in our plans. . . but the doctor wanted me to know.

It was such a sting to my soul every time a doctor would say those words. I should have been accustomed to hearing it. But the thought of not ever being a biological mother, not being able to experience carrying a baby in my womb, was devastating to say the least! I was a 24-year-old with no hope for marriage or children. I didn't think of Theo as my husband;

we were friends and bed partners only. Theo already had a daughter and two sons.

I loved my Tish Tish, my 1st goddaughter, and I loved all my other god children, but I wanted the experience of conceiving and giving birth, my teenage dream. I felt I was not a complete woman because I was barren. Four years later, I had another surgery through my navel (*laparoscopy*) to clean up more scar tissue and adhesions.

Throughout the years 1984-1988, I drank liquor, beer, wine, smoked cigarettes, got high from snorting cocaine, heroin, freebasing cocaine, and smoking marijuana. In the past, I used *hash* and marijuana laced with *"Angel dust"*–which I didn't like. I tried shooting up with heroin, preludes, taking *black beauties*, and *20/20's* (speed). Honestly, the cocaine made me feel good, but using needles was not my forté. So, I didn't do it again.

These are the things I did to relieve the pain and hurt I was feeling. It wasn't so much that it all felt good; it was my way of escaping my hurt, bad memories, everything I wanted to continue to forget. This was not and is not the answer to deal with problems. I thank God Almighty for sparing my life and my mind.

So, in truth, I contracted gonorrhea at a young age, being a victim of incest, rape and molestation, in which the venereal disease caused me to become barren. This was a lot for me to deal with! Therefore, I used drugs for mental pain relief. I was told by Butch and others that whenever I got tipsy, drunk, or high, all I talked about was having children. Crying a lot of times, I would ask, *"Why me? Why did God allow this to happen to me?"* I had no future, so I thought, and began wondering if

I was just created for abuse, misuse, hurt and pain? I felt sorry for myself; and these questions I wanted and needed answers to, even to want to live!

On one occasion, after making a drug run with Butch and Lorenzo, we decided to stay overnight at a hotel. While there, we smoked/freebased cocaine, which today is called *crack*. After a while, Lorenzo took a shower and said, Wow! That felt good!" He made it sound so refreshing I thought I would take a shower as well. So, I said, "Well, let me try it." I took a hot shower, when I got out and partially dressed, suddenly my heart started beating fast and I began to lose it. I started hyper-ventilating and couldn't really talk. I felt as if I was leaving this life, like my life was dwindling away. Butch and Lorenzo were talking to me, and Butch said, "Lie down and try to breathe slowly." But I was so scared, and it was hard to calm down.

Butch started praying for me (even though he was high). I believe Lorenzo was praying as well. All I could say in my mind and spirit was "Jesus." I knew there was power in the name of Jesus and that only He could help me: "Don't let me die like this! I don't want to go to hell! Jesus save me!" I thank God I soon came out of it and back to a regular heart rate.

Butch later explained that the heat caused me to start hy-perventilating after smoking because of my body temperature. From that moment on to this day, I never smoked or snorted again. My mind was made up to never use cocaine again. I was truly scared straight! I also realized I didn't want to die! Even though the pain was sometimes unbearable, I didn't know what was on the other side, especially being a backslider and not serving the Lord God as I was taught. I realized that living that type of lifestyle would not put me in the arms of Jesus. Instead, I was probably going to view the fiery dungeons of hell in torment. It was "game-over" for me after using cocaine. I thanked Butch and Lorenzo for praying and attending to me.

On our way home with a brick of cocaine in my purse we were speeding down the highway. Butch was driving, and I was in the back seat. Suddenly, we heard sirens behind us and there was much cause for concern. Lorenzo said, "Joyce give me the stuff; we won't let you catch a case if we are stopped." Fortunately, the cop passed us and was after someone else. Oh my goodness, I was really done with all the running, smoking and snorting! (Lol) That scared the (former language x#?&*) out of me! I take heed to warnings quickly! Jail is not a luxury, and God made a way of escape for all of us that day. Thank You, Jesus!

Butch nor Lorenzo never told anyone of this experience when we returned home; and this is the first time I have told this testimony of my miracle survival. Praise God again for not allowing the enemy (satan) to take me out! He didn't take me out when I tried to commit suicide because he didn't have God's permission, nor did he have it in that hotel.

Later, I learned that there was one particular prayer intercessor who shared with me that God had her praying for me, and I realized it was right around the same time of my encounter. You see there are people assigned to pray for you and, in their obedience, it can save a life, open up a door, or pave the way for a prayer request to be answered. God Almighty can only intervene in someone's situation *through prayer,* because He set it up this way.

Although I stopped using cocaine, I still smoked marijuana and drank beer, liquor, and wine. There was one occasion when I drank so much after leaving a club, I drove down a one-way street the wrong way and onto the sidewalk. Again, my brother Butch came down the street, took the keys away, and took me home. The next day I realized I could have been killed, killed someone, or put in jail. I never drove drunk again, tipsy but not drunk. There have been many incidents of my drinking to the point where I felt I was becoming an alcoholic, or beeraholic. I really didn't like it, but I didn't like how my emotions would overtake my mind either. Many times, I felt sorry for myself; for things I went through and was going through. Sometimes when I felt overwhelmed in my mind, drinking, and smoking calmed me and made me forget temporarily. A temporary fix was not what I needed; I needed a permanent solution.

It was one New Year's Eve, and I was home alone. I had stopped going out on New Year's Eve. Theo was at the private motorcycle club, and I had decided not to go with him. I sat on the couch with a beer, a joint and a cigarette, watching the countdown in Times Square. A voice in my spirit said, "If you don't stop the drinking you are going to die." I sat there and prayed for help, because it hurt, and I didn't know how to process what I heard in my head or my spirit. I fell asleep. The next day, New Year's Day, I went to a friend's house and, though I didn't really want any, I had a half glass of beer. I just didn't indulge like I normally would.

On Sunday, I woke up and called a friend from work who had been wanting me to visit her church. I asked her to pick me up; I would attend with her. Even though I was living an unsaved lifestyle, my upbringing was still speaking to me. The roots of my teaching, training, experiences and encounters of God Almighty, Jesus and Holy Spirit never left me. It was I who had left!

Sherry picked me up for the church service. I don't remember the message, but I remember when the preacher called for prayer. It felt like I was guided to the altar. I told the altar minister I wanted forgiveness and to be restored. When they prayed, I immediately started speaking in tongues! I felt the power of God descend upon me like rain and I couldn't help it and couldn't control it. I was once again talking to God. I felt so happy, light on my feet and fulfilled!

After the service, several people greeted me; they were all so warm and friendly. I remember telling a lady that she was going to have a baby. The words just came out. . . I felt a burning in my spirit to say, "God said, you're going to have a baby." What a new experience for me! As I write this, I am in awe of God. His ways are not our ways. I thought about how I gave her this news and yet I could not have a baby of my own, but I delivered that Word with joy. Wow! A few months after that, the same lady discovered she was pregnant and months later, she had a baby.

I told my friends and Theo that my life had changed. I stopped drinking, smoking marijuana and tried to stop smoking cigarettes. One thing at a time, that habit was a little difficult. . . I stopped for three months. It was when I had an encounter at the church that I began to allow the residue from the past to come in from old church hurts. Sherry thought it was her fault and didn't want blood on her hands, causing me to retreat and leave the church again. I assured her it was not her fault. Within four to six months, I was out again.

I couldn't deal with the spirit of rejection and jealousy because I was a musician. The choir wanted me to play, but the pastor's son who was also a musician, and won that battle. I also couldn't handle the pastor's attitude was toward me.

He never approached me, but I felt an uncomfortable, familiar spirit from my past, which I didn't give time to manifest. I hurried and left.

Again, satan had accomplished his goal for me to leave the church. Again, this happened because of thought suggestions in my mind and the situations happening. Instead of talking about the incident and how I felt, I just ran. . . left God and the church house altogether. The battlefield of my mind was neither armed nor dangerous.

Before leaving "church life," I had ended my intimate relationship with Theo; we still talked but there was no sexual activity going on. One late evening he called me and wanted to talk. I had been asleep and next thing I knew I heard a knock; he was at the door. I let him in, and we talked. And the next thing I knew we were in bed. As we indulged, I literally felt as if the Holy Spirit left my body. I promise! Fornication is a sin! We were not legally married!

Afterwards, I felt so bad because I realized I had grieved the Holy Spirit. The feeling of separation from the Holy Spirit is a terrible feeling to deal with. At that point, I made a conscious decision to let things go, including intimacy with Theo. I never went back to drinking or drugs. I was clean then and I'm clean now. Occasionally, I would have a glass of wine, but that was it. The desire and taste had left my tongue, my mind, and my spirit. I was delivered and made free from the unction to indulge.

By the time I had turned 30 my intimate relationship with Theo had resumed. I started thinking maybe I would adopt a child. Many of my friends had children; and I would babysit and have slumber parties with them. One of my sister-friends,

Linda, had no children, and we always ran the streets together. She couldn't understand why I always had everybody's child/children. I loved children and they made me feel like a mother..

Cina, one of my goddaughters, told me a few years ago (mid-2000's) that I was "a mother to many." That brought back a memory of a young lady from a sister church who would call me "Mom" when I was a teenager. And to this day she still calls me "Mom." While thinking about adopting I knew I had to prepare. I then put the thought aside and began to think about relocating to Atlanta. To this day, I don't remember exactly why I chose Atlanta. I knew it was a thriving city for Black entrepreneurs, but I don't recall the main reason. I now know it was a place God put in my spirit and mind.

I applied for a state job and got a letter requesting an interview. Pondering it, I realized that if I transferred and moved, I would give up the life I had really gotten used to, close friends I'd made, and leaving a man I had fallen in love with. Nevertheless, I had given up a life in the Motor City and moved to San Diego, returning a few months later because I didn't like it. But this was different now, because of Theo. After carefully considering everything, I decided not to pursue the opportunity.

When I turned 34, I started having more pain and my doctor said he would do another *laparoscopy* to clean adhesions and scar tissue. I knew the routine. After surgery, he assured me it had been successful, but said once again that I would never have children. With all the doctors I saw, I would still inquire. . . maybe looking for hope, yet accepting their prognoses. This specialist explained, a few years prior, why it was medically impossible for me to conceive.

He stated that the cilia [hairlike structures] in my one fallopian tube was destroyed from the *gonorrhea* they discovered. He drew a diagram showing me the feelers [cilia] and how they hold the egg for the sperm to fertilize it. My eggs dropped straight through the empty tube making it impossible for fertilization to happen. But he said something that I would later recall: "Although you can't have a child, I won't document it's impossible because I've seen miracles."

While doing the surgery, the doctor also discovered I had a tumor behind my uterus; he would monitor it because I was still too young for a hysterectomy. He told me if I started having pain or unusual symptoms to call him. I left the doctor's office and was a little saddened by his words. But on the other hand, I had gotten used to hearing that I would never conceive or give birth to my own child, so I started thinking again about adoption. I did a little research but never made the decision to move forward or to apply.

It had been a little over a month since the last surgery and I had transferred and been promoted to a new job with the State Public Aid Department, in the computer section for medical assistance and food stamps. I no longer worked with Theo. Although we didn't work in the same building, we still met for lunch.

One day I told my friend Ann (she worked in my building) that something was wrong because I had not had my monthly period. I concluded that the tumor must be getting bigger and now causing me not to have a cycle. Ann suggested that I call my doctor. I was scared and upset because I didn't want another surgery. After having four surgeries, I was tired of all the female problems! Most of my life I was sick and in pain. Even though I was upset, I didn't have the desire to get drunk or high; so finally, I called for an appointment. The day of the appointment I had made up in my mind it was okay to just go ahead and have the hysterectomy.

Ann was the only one who knew what was going on. The doctor's office staff did a routine urine pregnancy test before I was supposed to see the doctor. I noticed they were taking a long time to call me back, so I went to the desk to inquire, and the receptionist said she would check. After about five minutes she returned and called me to the desk to verify my name. "I am Joyce Moore," I said. Then she said, "Your urine test came back positive." My response was, "Oh you must have the wrong person because I can't have children." She looked again at the paper and verified my name and date of birth and then said, "Yes, the pregnancy test is positive, so you need to step over here and make an OB appointment."

At that moment I went into shock and the staff started asking if I was okay. "What's wrong? "Do you need to sit down?" All I remember is me saying, "I'm pregnant?" Apparently, a return appointment was scheduled, and I drove back to work. I was in a daze and my mind drew a blank as I drove back from the doctor's.

I remember walking into the office very slowly, getting to my desk and slowly sitting down. My co-workers started asking if I was okay because, according to them, I appeared pale. When I told them the news, they were happy for me, and the "Congratulations!" began, but I needed to process this. . . this news was unexpected and unbelievable! Then Dr. Russell's words came to me, and I pondered them: "Miracles do happen." Still in shock, I didn't feel I even deserved a miracle, or that God would do a miracle in my life and grant me a longtime request, my hope and dream. I believed in miracles, just not for me. I called Ann and told her the results and she laughed at me. . . but the laugh was on her, because a month later she found out she was pregnant!

After work when I went home, I sat down and just cried (happy tears), and thanked God for my miracle. Both a surprise and the best thing that could ever happen to me since receiving the Holy Spirit in my life. God had granted me the desire of my heart from long ago. I cried with joy! My friend Linda lived in the same building, and when I told her she was shocked as well. These friends had witnessed my pain, depression, alcohol and drug use while talking about the fact that I would never have children. The joy I felt was indescribable even to this day; nothing could ever take away the miracle and the joy God gave to me. Me, God did this for me! I'm crying with joy as I reflect on this miracle.

I waited until later that day to tell Theo. He had been there through all my surgeries and had heard the doctors say "no children" for me. He already had four children. I didn't know how he would react to me having his fifth child. I really wanted him to be happy for me, especially knowing all I had been through. When I told him he was just as shocked as I and needed time to process the news just as I did.

So, I took a leave of absence from my job to regroup and to take care of myself. I didn't tell Theo or too many people my plans. I didn't want anything to happen to me or my baby. Just wanted to be alone with no negative vibes or comments for the first 3 months. Someone moved my furniture into storage and then I moved to the outskirts of the city with two of our friends; they kept my temporary residence a secret.

While regrouping, I decided not to see Theo nor take his calls. I just wanted to remain calm, peaceful, and not have any mental issues that might cause me to miscarry. Yes, I was extremely overprotective! This was a miracle, and I would do whatever it took to protect us.

At my first follow-up appointment after receiving the news, and as I sat on the examining table, I heard Dr. Russell outside the door laughing somewhat. He walked in wearing his white doctor's jacket smiling and said, "I told you miracles do happen." He was so happy for me and reassured me not to worry about the delivery. With the pain I had been through, "labor should be a breeze" (my words, not his). During my pregnancy I was incredibly careful. Fortunately, I experienced no morning sickness.

During this time, my friend Cindra told me Theo wanted to talk to me and begged me to please call him. My buddy Alvin was also Theo's friend. He was very loyal to me and honored my wishes not to tell Theo where I was living, even though he disagreed with my decision. I knew this put him in a difficult position and I didn't want him to feel he wasn't loyal to his brother, but I needed him to keep my secret a little longer. After my first trimester, I moved closer into the city with Verne.

Cindra and Alvin continued begging me to call Theo, giving me some things to think about. No, I wasn't *trying* to hurt Theo, I just needed to take care of me, and my baby God gave me! Yes, I *was* being somewhat selfish and *only* thinking of me and my baby. A week after they both talked to me, I dropped my guard and called Theo. I could hear the concern and relief in his voice: we had been together for 10 years and now we were having a child, unexpectedly. I agreed to see him but at a public park.

We met and were happy to see each other. Three months had passed, and I was now showing. Theo explained his feelings and how we could move forward, assuring me that he would always be there for me and our baby. That night brought us back together and I was ready to let him be a part of our lives. We were both happy and talked about the future of our child.

I wanted a girl, but God already knew that was not what I needed. When I went for the ultrasound, the tech asked if I wanted to know the gender and before I could answer, I saw (smiling) it revealed! ◈ a boy! I already had a name either way. Theo was also happy about the coming birth of his third son. Had it been a girl, I would have been so overprotective because of my childhood and the issues with my father and other men. Like I said, God knew.

I enjoyed carrying my son, talking to him, praying for him, reading and singing to him. I loved him so much, my *gift* from God Almighty. Labor was "a breeze," for the pain I could bear. . . . Finally, he was here, and tears of joy flowed. Thank You, Lord, for this gift You've entrusted to me to raise as a king.

When my son was around 4 years old, I went for a checkup. The examination showed that the fibroid tumor had significantly increased in size and my doctor suggested surgery right away. He stated because I had been through so much and was now a little older, doing a complete abdominal hysterectomy would probably be in my best interest. Never again would I have to deal with any more pelvic pain, fibroids, or surgeries.

After having the surgery, I pondered the fact of never being able to conceive another child. There was a bit of sadness at first because of my childhood dream of having six children and a husband, and then I realized that although my dream was incomplete, I had been given an amazing and handsome gift from God, a treasure. I was satisfied.

Also, I realized I still had my goddaughters and godsons whom I loved as much as my own. I'm grateful to their parents who trusted me to co-parent their children. To this day I still welcome young men and women who adopt me as their spiritual mother (mother to many). My son accepts them as well and doesn't mind sharing.

One of my son's babysitters, a woman of great faith, adopted me as her *spiritual daughter* and my son as her *grandson*. She helped me in the area of having faith in God; trusting Him no matter what the situation looked like at the time. Her testimonies of what she endured were mind blowing and I started to believe more and more as God would prove Himself in various situations in my life. What I realized was that I believed God for others more than myself and my faith would waiver. I trusted in my abilities through my skills to provide for my son and myself. I had yet to experience total faith and trust in God Almighty.

I still wouldn't go to church, but I would read the Bible and listen to gospel music to help in times of trials. I thank Mother Webster for all she has done for me and poured into me. She was a true woman of God who believed as David, Abraham, Isaac and Jacob in God and His Word. Rest in Heaven Mother Webster, see you later.

Another of my son's babysitters was also a close friend and was heavily involved in her church. GG used to listen to Bishop Eddie Long and it was she who gave me a DVD to watch called "I Don't Need Delilah, I Need You" (which I didn't watch until months later). Her mother, belatedly known as "Honey," also played keyboards at their church. She welcomed me with open arms into her family and wanted us to collaborate on music. GG's dad was the assistant pastor and a very dedicated man of God. GG instructed the children, and she asked if my son could go with her to church when I worked. I was grateful because I wanted him brought up to know Jesus and praise Almighty God, even if I was slacking.

Finally, the question came when she invited me to come to church. I said, "Okay." It reminded me of some of our church services growing up. My son would get in the aisle and dance to the music, praising the Lord! To see this side of him at 4-years-old made me really happy. Eventually, I started attending more and more, helping to teach the choir. The pastor's daughter, who also played the organ, welcomed me to play as well, which helped me to start feeling a part of the congregation even though I wasn't a member.

Then it started happening: The pastor started calling me. . . checking on me and my son. I didn't think anything about it at first. Then my car went down, and Theo couldn't pick me up to go to work, so, the pastor offered to pick me up since he would be going in that direction. . . and just being nice as a pastor. He didn't do or say anything out of the way, but still I felt uneasy and sensed in my inner being (my spirit) that something was not right with this man.

The uneasiness I felt was from the years of abusive be-havior I had lived through; the fear and mistrust of religious men pretending to be true men of God but who had issues that were of the flesh, not the spirit of God. In my mind I thought: "This will never happen again. I'll take the bus if I have to, until my car is repaired." What a relief when we got to my workplace, and I got out of his car!

One night when GG was visiting my house, the phone rang, and I asked her to get it for me. It was her pastor. She questioned him because I had confided in her how I was feeling uncomfortable with him. He told her he was checking to see if everything was okay and she said, "Oh yeah! All is well." I didn't talk to him. I asked GG "Why is he calling me? He didn't need to check up on me. I was not a member of his congregation." I decided if he called again, I was going to let him have it!

GG said she would talk to her dad, who was the assistant pastor. When she told him about the situation, he spoke with me, and I told him how uncomfortable I felt. Either he could speak with him, or I would. Her father spoke with him and the next time I went to the church house, the pastor spoke to me but didn't linger on with a conversation. I stopped going. This was just too much for me. . . and I was not about to put myself in an uncomfortable situation.

I thought, I'm grown. . . and I will cuss (not curse) him out and physically hurt him if he attempted to touch me. I had changed, I was not the timid and quiet little girl or teenager any longer. This made me even more distant from attending church services, just what satan wanted. But at that time, I didn't realize or understand the spiritual warfare I encountered was to keep me from returning or getting closer to God Almighty and letting Jesus be Lord over my life.

Pastors or church leaders, I just didn't want to deal with or have anything to do with them. Just didn't want to have a conversation with them or be in their presence, especially when I got a feeling that they were not real or up to no good! Just like the song *Smiling Faces Sometimes* says, "smiling faces show no traces of the evil that lurks within" (The Undisputed Truth, 1971).

I needed to get back to fellowshipping with believers. I knew this truth, and a part of me was being drawn back to what I was raised to believe and embrace, Jesus, my personal Savior, and getting closer to the Almighty God. I just didn't want to deal with preachers, pastors, church shenanigans, charades, or religiosity. I felt there was more to God than what I knew.

In late 1998, I began having money problems and couldn't understand why. I worked for the State Government and made a decent salary, but it had become "more month than money." GG's dad told me that if I *tithed*, God would supply my needs and referenced biblical Scriptures: Malachi 3:10 (NKJV), Philippians 4:13 and Luke 6:38. These Scriptures proved to be true later in my journey.

There was a point in my life when it seemed as if God was *blowing on my money*. I use that term now, but then it was more like it just disappeared. I just could not manage and didn't know what was going on! As stated earlier, I made good money working for the Department of Revenue and yet I was struggling. God always supplied our needs, but still, I had barely enough, with no wiggle room.

So, I started paying tithes but still didn't see any significant change. Looking back now, I must admit my trust and faith in the Word of God was not where it should have been. I didn't realize I had to mix belief and faith with my act of giving. For instance, I would give and still worry about money. True trust and belief eliminate worry. I needed to get to the place where there was no doubt in my mind that God was going to work things out for my good and His glory! It took years for me to grasp and understand true trust, belief and having faith in God and His Word.

One day I was home, and my son was with his godparents. I began to talk to God, praying, and I broke down and told Him I didn't want to live my life, die, and go to hell. I confessed the hatred in my heart; that I knew I needed to forgive, not hate, people who had done me wrong, but I didn't know how to release the hatred and move on. I didn't know how to be free from the past, live for the now, and look forward to a bright future.

My birthplace was a town I hated, which included strong dislike and/or hatred of people such as my dad, many of the church people, pastors, and those in leadership. (Others in my life who were not from my birthplace and had done wrong to me, I had forgiven. . . didn't think about them any longer.) I cried and prayed for quite a while. Then I heard a still whisper of a voice that seemed to be inside me, but wasn't me, say, "Go back to where it started." I said, "Huh?" "Go back to where it started"... "Back to MTV? Oh no, for real?" I asked, not really understanding the answer.

However, I sat down and thought about it; thought about my job, about Theo, taking my son away from his father, my friends, and my life in the capital city. Then again, He said, "You must go back to where it started," and I began having a peace about it. I thought, *well, if I must go, I will go to get peace, and not end up in hell.* I told God "I don't know how to forgive, but I'll go" my first decision to be obedient to God.

Theo didn't understand when I told him. I tried explaining that I was at a place in my life where I desired to be fully restored to God. I wanted Jesus to be the Center of my life! I wanted to get right, stop hating, stop fornicating, stop doing things that didn't please the Lord. I told him I had to face my past and get healed. He was not happy but didn't fight my decision. It took me a few weeks to move on with my decision, for it seemed as if God started blowing *more* on my money. So, finally I resigned from my job and moved to MTV after my son's school year ended in 1999.

This was one of the hardest decisions and moves I have ever made. The devil tried to talk to my mind with seeds of doubt and a truck load of *what ifs.* I thought I was going to be the most miserable person in the world, and I knew I couldn't show my feelings to my son. He understood we were moving, and that his dad was not moving with us. But we were able to spend a lot of time with Theo for a few months before school was out.

My last intimate encounter with Theo was June 12, 1999. To this day in 2023, as I am finishing this book, I have not been with a man, woman, animal, sex toy, or my own self (for anyone who is thinking about masturbation). It takes Almighty God, Jesus, and the Holy Spirit to keep a person celibate along with a made-up mind. I take no credit for achieving celibacy. I have not had many men approach me since surrendering my whole life to Almighty God. It's as if I've been hidden from men attempting to be in a relationship with me, and it's okay. I know that when I'm ready (by God's standard) for my king, my husband, my destiny mate, he will find me, his missing rib.

Do I get lonely? Not really, and it's because I stay so busy with the Kingdom of God and the businesses, He has given me to attend. There's no time to dwell on being alone. I do sometimes think about it - intimacy with a man - and sadness will try to come, but I snap out of it and say, "God help me not to think about this right now, in your timing, I trust You." Then I focus my thoughts on my work, career and my God-given vision concerning my life. My husband will come, I know, and it won't be too late to enjoy each other.

Tip: Flee all temptation! Don't put yourself in a situation to be tempted and don't play with temptation.

Chapter 5

Taking Me Back

Peonies Represent Returning

Back to Where It All Started

It was nearing the time to depart for MTV. The Saturday we left, my relatives arrived to pick up my son and me and drive us to southern Illinois. In my mind and heart, I just knew I would be back as soon as I forgave people whom I held a grudge for, or simply hated. The Lord told me I would not always be living in MTV, that it was temporary. Of course, I took that to mean I would be moving back to the capitol city. Little did I know my life was about to change in a way I would have never dreamed.

Upon arrival at MTV, my family was filled with excitement for the move and to have me closer. I still believed that I would be miserable and unhappy, but to my surprise and total shock, I was content. When God has you and you are in His will, it's unexplainable how much peace He gives you in a life-changing situation. After being there a few weeks, it wasn't as bad as I thought it would be and I was so grateful. God loves you and me, and He doesn't do things to cause us to be unhappy and discontented. I missed my family and friends in the capital city, including Theo, but I was where I was supposed to be at this time in my life. My son was happy, even though he missed his dad and friends. But he was able to start bonding with his other family members and make new friends. And if he is with me, he is going to be happy.

Jobs

Now, before moving to MTV, I had been looking for a job. One of my cousins worked at a car dealership in MTV and assured me I would have a job waiting for me. I sent in my resume and all I needed to do was come. When I got there and inquired about the position, I was told there was no position available; and I was overqualified. *Overqualified?!* I didn't understand this lingo because I had never heard it, since having been on my job with the State of IL for over 20 years. This floored me and I was quite upset. No job. I needed to provide for my child. I had money saved but it wouldn't last forever.

We lived with my mother and grandmother. My mom lived with my grandmother who had a big home. My grandfather purchased this big brick home, and it was paid for long before he passed; Mom had moved in with my grandmother after he passed. Even though there was more than enough room, I was used to my own house and my own space, and I knew I would need a job to acquire my own place, to supply our personal needs. I also knew I could go back to the capital city and get my job back, but it wasn't the will of the Lord. I was in a hard place.

The year is 1999. I started applying for jobs and my resume intimidated employers, but I couldn't dumb it down. My experience and skills were "as is" period. Prayer works. I prayed and soon I got a call for a job paying approximately $5.25/hr. I was so humiliated because I'd come from making $15/hr. This was a slap in the face! But I humbled myself and took it because I needed a job.

Folks, I worked at Walmart. Now my attitude was good and at first, I looked at it like *I was starting over.* It was a job, a new field, a new experience, though a somewhat embarrassing time in my life. I did think about how my capital city friends would react to my dropping $28,000 in salary; however, it's all in how you perceive a situation when making a God move. I didn't realize it then, but I did later: God's plan for my son and I was not the plan I had in mind for us, but I surrendered to His plan and His way and pressed through the embarrass-ments, going to work with a smile. And not long after, I got a breakthrough!

Struggles come to grow you and stretch you to become the person God wants you to be, for a purpose designed by Him. However, when you're in the test/struggle, it's real and you don't see the end result while living or going through it if you haven't reached that level of faith and trust in Almighty God. When I shifted my mindset to realize God was still pro-viding, and I started thanking Him instead of looking at it in a negative way, things changed.

A data entry company called me to come in for an inter-view; this was more in my field. Remember, I began data entry/keypunch back in 1976 in Detroit, so I was happy to accept it and with a higher pay of $6.25/hr. I worked there for a few months without complaining and soon got another offer at an internet company as an account clerk, managing billing and other accounting duties. It paid $7.50/hr. I was moving on up in this small town. I now earned half of what I was earning when I worked for the State Government. After working there for nearly 15 months, the company was bought out and I was offered to either transfer or take severance pay and collect un-employment. The transfer was to Oakland, CA, and I was not moving! God had brought me back on assignment; I knew that was not an option for me. I had to stick to His plan.

A few months later I got a job working for a cellular company paying $9 an hour. It lasted a year until I got fired for not having a home phone to cover the weekend shift. The supervisor knowingly scheduled me for the weekend when I was moving into another home. Needless to say, the un-employment office granted me approval for payment because of that ridiculous reason. I received unemployment pay until I was hired as the lead bookkeeper at a TA truck stop. I liked this job. It was a new position of which I had no experience, but it became a strong part of me and my future.

I counted money up to $100,000 a day, prepared deposits for Brinks, and balanced cash flow of the store, shop, restaurant, and an additional fast-food chicken restaurant. In 2006, I resigned with the intention of moving to Atlanta, GA. I am so grateful for the experience and the people I worked with for over 3 years.

Resigning and not making the move now left me without a job; so, I started looking again, but it took a minute to get a "good" job assignment. Seeing me struggling financially, my mom suggested moving back in with her and my grandmother. My son and I moved back to the grandmas' house, and I started taking care of their business and organizing their finances. This was the beginning of my training for what I was to do in the future. By then, I was in the early stages of my entrepreneurship. I always had a way of making income; I just needed to make more.

The move to Atlanta didn't happen because I was not prepared; my measure of faith was not enough to take a leap that seemed crazy or out of the box. I was still counting on my abilities and skills to take care of my son and me. I didn't trust God to supply all my needs as He promised in His Word. I knew He could, but I held back with self-doubt. I could and would minister and encourage others that God is true to His Word, saying, "Just have faith and trust Him." I believed it for others, not for myself. God had to help me to learn He was and is my only Source no matter what the situation may be in my life.

Soon, I was hired to work for a nonprofit organization as a finance assistant to the CFO and product manager. The pay now was $13.75/hr., and benefits were good. I worked there for over three years until that organization merged with another one and moved to another city. Again, another move was offered to me near St. Louis, MO and, again, that was not an option for me.

While still working for a nonprofit, during my off time, I began helping a bottled water company transition their business from paperwork bookkeeping to using QuickBooks. The owner, Patty, would work for hours day in and day out sending out handwritten invoices manually, and using physical ledgers to keep daily transactions. My mother introduced her to me when I moved to MTV and told her all my skills. One day while at the water company, Patty told me her problem and asked if I could help. I said "Yes" and went to work setting up her business in QuickBooks.

I created a mini manual with pictures to teach her how to create and print invoices, enter banking information, receive payments and other necessary tasks. Patty was an older woman and had no computer skills and was learning to type from a teaching CD. Patty learned and followed the manual and became a pro. She told me I was her *angel* sent by God. *This too was an assignment.*

God opened another job assignment with a small insurance company ($13.65/hr.) after the nonprofit job closed. I was hired as the bookkeeper and worked there for almost a year until the owner sold her business. I realized that I had "assignments"; that God placed me in jobs not for just the money, but for ministry and the demonstration of Christ in my life. I was to demonstrate Jesus in my mountain of influence by showing and sharing the love of Jesus to whomever would listen and receive.

Looking back, I sometimes would get frustrated with these jobs, but there were certain people within each business I was assigned to help. They shared that my presence impacted their lives, that I helped to change their lives for the better. I was so happy and filled with joy when one of the ladies, who had been struggling, decided to receive Jesus into her heart and the Lord beautifully saved her. I love leading people to Christ! Problems don't just go away, but having Jesus in your life will help you deal with the situations that arise. He gives us the assurance that everything will be alright, if we just believe, have faith, and receive.

Chapter 6

The Faces of Forgiveness & Deliverance

White Tulips, Yellow Rose
& Purple Hyacinth
All Represent Sorry, Regret & Forgiveness

Forgiveness - 1

If I had not returned to the place where it all started, I would never have been a spiritual influence on the people I met. They saw Christ in me through my struggles and triumph. I had to trust God, take Him at His Word and allow Him to help me forgive those who had wronged me. Forgiveness is hard if your mind is stuck on the past hurts. I made a choice to allow God to change my heart and give me the desire to forgive.

I, on my own – in my flesh (soul) – did not want to forgive these people. But once I prayed and said to the Lord, "Not my will, but Your will be done in my life," things began to change in my mind. I gave God permission to change me, change my mindset and my heart. I didn't fight against Him. Only God knows when a person is ready to truly forgive and leave the past behind. I believed it would happen and waited. . . not knowing when or how the process would take place.

In my experience, forgiveness is miraculous! Something that takes place in the heart, mind, and soul, which only God can do with our permission. God gives us *free will* and we can choose our path. I chose for Him to change me to want forgiveness to take place, and He answered my prayer because that is what He wanted as well. Once I surrendered my will to God, His desire became my heart's desire. This is truly miraculous to me. I was now ready to forgive my dad. I had anxiety around how and when it would happen, but I felt God was going to do it in His perfect timing.

One day, my niece Delilah was with me in my living room and asked, "Auntie, when are you going to talk to Granddad so you can move back, and I can come on my visits?" I answered, "I don't know, I don't know if I'm ready." I went into the kitchen and the next thing I knew she was handing me the phone. In my spirit I knew who was on the other end but wasn't sure what to do. I asked her who it was, and she didn't say. . . she just gave the phone to me.

I opened my mouth and said, "Hello". . . on the other end a long-ago familiar voice said, "Hello, who is this?" I responded, "This is your daughter." I was totally numb on the inside! He responded, "Oh, which one?" And before I could answer he named all my other sisters and I said, "No, this is Joy." His response was a shock to my inner being: "Oh my God! I have been wanting to talk to you for 15 years and ask for your forgiveness. I am sorry. I was a terrible father and did terrible things, and I am so sorry, forgive me."

Immediately, when those words hit the atmosphere I felt the tears, and felt a weight lift off my shoulders as if heavy armor had been taken off me! I felt lighter in my body and spirit. Emotionally, there was no hatred, no animosity, nor sadness. I could remember everything and every event, but felt no painful emotions with the memories. I told him I forgave him, and to this day we have never talked about what happened in my childhood. He let me know that he had received Jesus as his Lord & Savior and how God had changed him for real.

We spoke on the phone for a long while; it was as if I had just met my real father as an adult. I was so overjoyed that God had miraculously taken away my heavy-loaded emotional burden and could barely contain myself after that call! I thanked my niece for allowing God to use her to initiate the healing of my soul on my way to being made whole. I was so excited to share this testimony, but I didn't say anything until we had Bible Study the next night. I was still so overjoyed and free that when I told it, the anointing of God came over me and people rejoiced with me, especially those who knew my story (not too many). But the Holy Spirit is contagious! I danced before the Lord and was filled with joy and happiness! I tell you, I was on a spiritual high, not to be compared to a fleshly high ◈this high lasted a long time and the *joy of the Lord* is still in my heart today! Words cannot explain it! I felt like preaching!

When you choose to forgive, the freedom that overshadows you is unexplainable. It is so hard to describe how I felt because it is an experience, an encounter that refreshes your mind, soul, and spirit. I want to impress upon you who are reading this book or listening by audio, that God is real! Jesus is real! Holy Spirit is real! When you decide to surrender your will over to God, you can be free!

Later, people began asking questions about how I would feel if I saw him. Would I ask questions or bring up the past? Would I still feel forgiveness since talking on the phone is one thing, but seeing the person who hurt you face to face may be different? Well, I believe in my heart that when God does a miraculous work, it is solid; a done deal that cannot be undone. But at the time, I could only say, "I don't know how I would react." I only knew that true forgiveness is never bringing the incident up to the one who hurt you, the past painful acts or deed(s) done to a person or by a person, because it is dead. All is forgiven and put in the sea of forgetfulness; read *Micah 7:19, Isaiah 43:18 and Philippians 3:13-14 NKJV.*

I have journeyed many years with unforgiveness. To experience freedom is something we all can experience. Mine came at a time in life when I was at a crossroad: I was okay where I lived with a good job, house, a child, friends, and a man I loved. The problem was that I lacked a close and holy relationship with Jesus, with God Almighty. I was still living a sinful life of fornication and unforgiveness in my heart. The Bible plainly says no sin will enter Heaven and many **lifestyles** of sin will not inherit the Kingdom of God. See I Corinthians 6:9-10. I am not saying we won't sin, because *all have sinned and fall short of God's glory* (see Romans 3:23 NKJV). However, there is a difference between committing sin and living a lifestyle of sin.

From my upbringing and reading the Bible, I knew I could not enter the Kingdom of God with hatred in my heart, a lifestyle of fornication, and never get married (sex is meant *only* for the husband and wife); see Genesis 2:24 KJV, and Hebrews 13:4 NKJV. I had to make the decision to stop living a sinful lifestyle. I had to make a choice to go with the decision of obedience to God and resign from my job (with only 10 more years until early retirement), give up my nice home, leave my friends, end my relationship with my son's father, and return to where it all started, a small town that I really despised.

When I look back, I would not change my decision; this was all part of God's plan for my life, my divine destiny, my Kingdom of God inheritance, His promises being manifested, and my best life healed and whole. I have no regrets.

My God Relationship

God knew how I felt about preachers/leadership in the church, so he placed me under the leadership of my brother. I was prepared for his ministry because while in the capitol city my sister-in-law had been sending me the messages he preached. When I first heard him, it was as if he had been preaching for years. When we were young children, we used to play sermon albums of various preachers and mock them by memorizing their words and preaching with them. But this was real! As I listened to him teach and preach, I could feel the anointing, the presence of God.

Before I moved to MTV, my friend, her family, and I would travel just to be in the worship services there. They loved him and how God used him to deliver the Word of God. The worship service was off the chain!!! PG is also a musician, as I mentioned, and so devoted to God that the worship and praise put a person in the glory zone. Once a month he would have a night of worship called "Fresh Fill." I had not experienced the presence of God like this in years. We traveled for this service, not knowing that God was preparing me and breaking things off and out of me, until that day God spoke to me to leave the capitol city. I believe I was set up by God!

My brother's messages gave me revelation of how simple it is to serve God and receive Jesus as Lord and Savior. It was as if the Scriptures came alive! I wanted to know God in a more real way. I knew there had to be more to God than just the routine of going to church, serving in a ministry, getting saved, speaking in tongues, dancing, singing, shouting, and getting others saved. Where was the part about the Kingdom of God and it being on earth as it is in Heaven? I was about to start on a journey that would reveal God and all His promises.

One evening while still in the capital city, I went to see a play at a church. It was called "Heaven's Gate & Hell's Flames" and I was not surprised by the theme because I knew about Heaven and Hell but was estranged from God. By the time the play was over, I was in tears. There was an altar call and, mind you, I was raised to believe that to be saved you must speak in tongues. Well, a pastor who did the altar call invited those who wanted to receive Jesus Christ as Lord and Savior to do so by repeating these words... a prayer of repentance that went something like this: *Father God, I confess with my mouth and believe in my heart that Jesus died on the cross, was buried, and rose from the dead on the 3rd day for my sins. Jesus, come into my heart and be Lord over my life and because I confess and believe, I am saved"* (see Romans 10:9 NKJV).

Now in my mind I'm thinking, that is so simple, and they didn't say you need to tarry for the Holy Ghost, speak in tongues and you'll be saved. I was now confused because there were 100's of people who went to the altar to receive Jesus as Lord and Savior and to be saved. They asked whoever said the *prayer of salvation* to follow the altar ministers to another room. When I got back there, I was greeted with such kindness and felt genuine love. The minister I spoke with welcomed me and I filled out a card with my information and they gave me material and a Bible and instructed me to get into a good Word-based church. I then left. What just happened?

I was with friends, and I felt confused; they were not. But you know God will not leave you confused, for He is not the creator or author of confusion. I listened to a cassette tape of my brother ministering (that my sister-in-law sent) and on it, he was explaining the plan of salvation from Romans 10:9 NIV. Immediately, God brought revelation to my mind; opened the understanding of His Word, His plan of salvation. Receiving salvation was separate from receiving the Holy Ghost or Holy Spirit with the evidence of speaking in tongues. It was so plain to me, the confusion left. I was in awe and the Holy Spirit spoke to me: *It is not hard to be saved and God does not make anything hard.* I was so excited that this revelation was made available to me! It's funny how God will open your mind to understand the Scriptures.

Why would He make salvation hard to receive? Remember when waiting to receive the baptism of the Holy Spirit with the evidence of speaking in tongues (our heavenly language), it's a promised gift (see Acts 2:38-39). I strongly suggest that you read Acts 2, explaining the day of Pentecost and the Holy Spirit. We do need both, plus the baptism in water making a public declaration of a life-changing experience, repentance of sins, burying the old you, and coming up a new you.

Although I was first baptized at age 9, I got baptized again after moving back to MTV. I felt I needed to do this act again now that I had a better understanding and had rededicated my life to God after twenty years of being a prodigal child.

It was one Sunday that I decided to be baptized, having previously discussed it with my brother who would baptize me. Remembering the experience of receiving the Holy Ghost back in my teens, this experience was so awesome and powerful that I get so much joy thinking about it! I had a different mindset. I prayed that God would do *something new* when I went down in the water; that I would come up a *new person* in mind, soul, and spirit.

My brother, the pastor, took me under the water and when I came up my feet felt light. . . I started dancing in the water. . . speaking in *new tongues* that I'd never experienced or heard. They helped me out of the water, and I fell to my knees, still speaking in tongues. I lay on the floor prostrate and heard several languages as I spoke. I heard Chinese, French, Dutch, African, Aramaic, etc. I recall these because I heard *in the spirit*. This was the most profound Holy Ghost experience I ever had since I had returned to God. I felt like a brand-new person.

Scriptures are true! The Bible says, *"Train up a child in the way he should go: and when he is old, he will not depart from it"* (Proverbs 22:6 KJV) I am living proof of this Scripture, for I came back to my roots after encountering the life of a heathen. God is so merciful and forgiving. I thank Him for His grace. A great change had come over me and the joy of the Lord was all in me, even the more.

Forgiveness - 2

Church leadership hurt me deeply. I had forgiven my dad, but was unsure about leadership, the pastor who took my real virginity, the pastor who teased me about my sickness, and the pastor who kissed me with his tongue going in my mouth. These were "men of God" that I needed to - had to - forgive. As I've mentioned, God strategically had me under my brother's leadership, and I didn't know how it would happen, but I purposed in my heart to forgive them. It seemingly came very slowly. However, looking back, it was all in God's timing, not mine.

The pastor who teased me was the first to apologize. It happened when I was visiting the old church where I grew up. He loved to call people out from the pulpit. I was sitting in service, and he caught my eye while he was talking, and I knew the look I gave him sent a message. It was saying "If you do, I will...." It was a look of dislike and disgust; a threatening look because that was what I felt on the inside. He left it alone and moved on with the service.

During worship, the Holy Spirit convicted me, and I felt bad. So after service, I went to his office and asked if I could talk to him. He agreed, and I began telling him the reason I treated him the way I did: "When I was growing up, you teased me about being sick and I was really sick." I told him "I didn't appreciate it and was hurt, mad and hated to come into this church. . . I wanted to apologize for how I had looked at him." Continuing to say, "When I left and moved to Detroit, I later got sick again and found out I had a disease, *gonorrhea*, which I had for many years, and it was from rape." I told him how it destroyed my tubes to the point I was barren, until God changed it to allow me to have a son. He began to weep, saying he didn't know and that he was sorry. That was a great relief for me and for him. I remember staying overnight with his family back then and when that started happening, I no longer wanted to go there. Once again, God allowed the miraculous to happen we hugged, and all is well to this day. We have not discussed this past event because it's over. We have moved forward.

Forgiveness – 3

The kissing pastor, it was not as hard to forgive him even though he was wrong for doing what he did during a church service. I was not the only young girl he had done this to. This hurt wasn't as deep as the other hurts but added more distrust in pastors and leadership. He would often see me or speak with me outside of a church event. My g-sis Esther would tell me he asked about me and we all met for lunch a couple of times. I had already forgiven him and let it go, after God had done so much for me through the other two encounters of forgiveness. When I decided to let it go, God honored my decision and removed the emotional scar this man caused.

Forgiveness – 4

This man of God was anointed and appointed by God, with no denying it. The young people loved him. He hurt many and used many, but this book is about my experience, so I won't reveal those of anyone else. I did not and could not understand how he could operate under the power of God and commit such horrible acts with an underage child. It took years for me to understand gifts and callings are without repentance (*see Romans 11:29 AMP*). God gives us all gifts and we are called or destined for God's Kingdom, yet a person can and will commit sins and not turn away from it while operating in the gift or call.

The devil used this man and tried to destroy my life many times because of the sexual immoralities. God's grace and mercy was upon us both. I couldn't see it while in the storm, but I now know it. This man stole my ability to conceive (so the devil thought), according to the medical records ◈ but God received the glory in the end!

I had not seen this man in over 20 years, and he had since been elevated to the title of "apostle." Now, he was the last pastor from the past I needed to forgive. I wanted a verbal apology and also thought with it, there would be an explanation of *why* he did what was done to me. My questions were: *Why did you desire a teenager over your wife? Why me?* In my heart, I felt I wasn't the only one but, being one of the girls, *why would you do this as a man of God pastoring two churches?* He never answered these questions, and never will.

The Apostle was coming into town to the church where I was raised, where he once pastored and committed these horrible things to me. Because no one knew about the rape, they expected me to be happy and excited that he was coming to preach. I struggled in my mind with going to face this man. Thoughts of what I would do. . . how would I react? Will I want to hurt him? Will he apologize? And do I even want to put myself through these emotions? I prayed about it, and suddenly a boldness and peace came over me to face my giant. Although I was nervous, I decided to go. Something inside me stood up as if I were indestructible. What could he do to me? I was grown, an adult, and in control of my life, as well as having the help of Almighty God on my side.

The night came. I had been a little anxious or nervous, but I was determined to go and behold this man again. His wife also accompanied him. I remembered her as a quiet and bitter person (which I guess she had every right to be in my opinion). It was during praise and worship that the man of the hour walked in. He was older looking, of course, and grayer with a beard. His wife was different, too, she had a smile on her face and seemed to have changed. I could see she was happier since I last saw her many years prior. My stomach had a little ache, but I didn't feel hate in my soul. I felt nothing; it was as if I was unemotional. I just stared at him and when he preached, I sat and listened while people were engaged and emotional.

The Word of God was on point, but the deliverer was the man who took my virginity and caused me to have years of pain from a venereal disease that could have taken my life, a disease that caused sterility and my inability to have children. These thoughts ransacked my mind, emotions, and soul. I had to fight my thoughts and call on Jesus to help me, so that I would not regress into an emotional and traumatic state. I wanted an acknowledgment and apology. God did help me.

After the service, I was talking to others whom I had not seen for a while. I don't exactly remember who it was, but one of my family members asked, "Oh, this is Joyce. Do you remember her?" This man looked at me as if he barely remembered me and replied, "Oh yeah, I remember anointing her hands when she was playing the organ." He then proceeded to ask me how I was doing? I recall feeling like the scum of the earth and used, like a person who was involved in a one-night stand. It really hurt because he had taken so much from me and seemed to not care or remember not just the encounters, but not remember me. What a slap in the face! I spoke and then walked away.

I thank God for Jesus and His saving grace, because if this had happened prior to me returning to God, I would have cussed him out and exposed everything, saying: "You don't remember me? How dare you!" This has been a hard valley to walk through. I've had to fight my mind and embrace the fact that I need to continue to pray and think differently.

Many of the family and a few friends wanted to go eat together. After the church service, we gathered at a restaurant and the Apostle came, along with his son-in-law, who was a Bishop. We had grown up together in the same church; and his son in law discerned that something was wrong with me by the look on my face, as well as no conversation. I got up and went to the bar (not for an alcoholic drink but for a soda), and the son-in-law Bishop Williams followed me to ask what was wrong.

I decided to tell him and asked that he keep it to himself. I told how I was disgusted and felt awful, because this Apostle acts as if he just met me and never had a relationship with me. He talked to me for a minute and gave me words of wisdom, and I felt better. . . at least I wasn't going to make a scene. But have you ever had a heat feeling come over you with a desire in your belly that just wanted to make a scene ◈ even if you were going to be sarcastic? That was the point I was at; and I had to really fight and pray within not to say anything, because I wasn't that quiet little girl that wouldn't speak up back in the day.

No, if I had not been saved and seeking to walk like Jesus, I would have cussed him out and exposed him. I thank God Almighty that I had matured enough in Him to hold my peace and be quiet. As children of God, we must respect the callings of the five-fold ministry and touch not the anointed and do them no harm, but that was not in my mind whatsoever. I respect the position but not the man who violates and uses his authority to hurt people because of the position.

We said our farewells and went home. I thanked God for getting me through that night of a most dreadful reunion with my enemy, and I say that because anyone who hurts you intentionally is an enemy. I asked God to help me forgive him from my heart. This was a fight that I needed to win. As I forgave the other two, I needed to truly forgive him. My fight with honoring and dealing with leadership had become a burden and a challenge. I needed a breakthrough, emotionally and spiritually. I respected people in leadership roles but did not trust them, period.

The second time I saw the Apostle was at an event in St. Louis, MO. I went with my sisters and others to a church ministry anniversary celebration. He was the guest speaker and was anointed in delivering the Word of God. (I thought maybe this time there would be an apology and memory recall.) After service he greeted my sisters and friends and only said "Hello" to me, as if I were a stranger. From that point, I decided, *forget it, this man is not going to recognize me or apologize to me.* I said in my mind: *God help me to forgive him.* From that night going forward I dismissed it from my mind. Maybe he remembered but refused to acknowledge or maybe he chose a long time ago to wipe it from his memory. I don't know, only God knows. I had to move forward and put it out of my mind for now.

Forgiveness is a decision as well as an act of faith. Without the faith to believe in God, forgiveness will not happen. I had to say to God, "I forgive him" and allow God to change my heart and take away the pain and sting of those memories. Again, a miracle.

Journey to Deliverance

Under the leadership of my brother, I began growing by leaps spiritually, and I was thirsty for more. I was stepping into another realm of God and my hunger increased.

I attended a conference called P.I.P. (Pentecost in Perspective). The late Bishop Norman L. Wagner, its founder and host, was an incredible and powerful man of God with whom I immediately connected in the spirit. He taught and preached what I was thinking and longing for in God. It was the most amazing experience I had ever had in a church setting.

I recall two others who preached a Word that was pertaining to me and that stayed with me: Bishop Noel Jones and the late Apostle Bishop Eddie L. Long, who would later become my spiritual father. It was he whom my friend and babysitter GG introduced me to by video when I lived in the Capital City.

Bishop Noel Jones preached a message that is still in my heart today: "I'm Qualified." And I met him in the hallway when I went to purchase the DVD; the first high-profile man of God I had met since returning to the church. I had never heard of him or any other high-profile men of God because when I left the church world, I truly left (Lol). I then started following the ministries of both Bishop Jones and Bishop Long... they helped me to grow more spiritually.

Years prior, my brother and his wife attended P.I.P. conferences and they would drop their three children off in the Capital City for me to watch while they were away. Back then, I never inquired about the conference or had any interest in ever attending. Funny how life turns out (Lol). Never did I imagine I would attend several conferences of P.I.P. God has a way of bringing things together and in perspective.

In 2004 one of my sisters and I attended a Singles Conference at New Birth, in Lithonia, GA. I had been listening to the pastor and host, Bishop Long, since P.I.P. ◇something in his voice made my spirit leap. He had a sound! The Sunday after the conference I decided I was going to attend the 1st service. The message he preached hit me; it was titled "Should I Wait Another Day."

When the service was over, I was still crying when a lady approached me and asked, "If I was a first lady and were the two women next to me my armor bearers?" I told her I wasn't and that I had just met these women (from England). Then the lady began talking directly to me, telling me things about myself no one knew but me and God. This was the first prophecy I ever had. God didn't allow preachers or leaders to prophesy to me, and I believe it was mainly because I didn't believe and would not receive the prophecies because I did not trust preachers and leaders. My thing was *don't get close ever again.*

After the lady finished speaking, she gave me instructions to get in line and get the anointing [impartation] from Bishop Long. She asked the ladies about accompanying me and they agreed and, with one on each side, we proceeded into the hallway where Bishop Long was greeting people. I was still in awe. . . tears were flowing down my cheeks. . . and both ladies were praying as we walked. When we reached a certain point in line the security cut it off at me. Immediately, the devil came to steal my word seed. The security explained Bishop Long had to get upstairs to prepare for the next service. I was so confused. I told the ladies they were dismissed; I thanked them and gave them a hug.

Meantime, my cousin was there to pick me up and his girlfriend was with him. I must have looked puzzled because he asked what was wrong and I explained how I was instructed to get in line and meet Bishop Long. Cousin's girlfriend said, "I know Tom; I'll go ask him to let you meet Bishop Long." She turned and went in the direction to talk to Tom and as she approached Tom, Bishop Long was coming toward me and my cousin. He spoke and hugged me, and while he was hugging me I said, "May God restore virtue to you." And he said, "I receive it." When the girlfriend came back, she said we could meet him. But God wanted me to see that the Words from the lady were from Him; and the instructions were as well. The Lord allowed me to see how He works behind the scenes.

Also, my obedience set in motion the instructions from His prophet that manifested right before my eyes. Now, I don't know what that *first lady stuff* was about, but I do know the Lord used that lady to point me in the direction of my divine journey, my destiny. That day changed my life! When I returned to MTV, I was more hungry for God. I read, listened, and studied with New Birth, with Bishop Jones and others, including Bishop Norman L. Wagner.

In 2006, I attended *Megafest,* a conference hosted by Bishop T.D. Jakes. Bishop Long was there promoting his new book, "It's Your Time"; my goddaughter and I bought a book (he would be signing books after a session we attended). Cina and I went to get our books signed and happened to be the first in the signing line, so he took pictures with us. He asked where we were from and I replied, Illinois, adding that I was thinking about moving to Atlanta but was unsure. He spoke words to me that I live by to this day: "Whenever you have peace in your spirit, you will know it's the right move." Then he asked to pray for me. This was my second meeting with Bishop Long.

I returned home and started streaming New Birth services regularly ◈I was a *virtual member* back then! In 2007 I told my brother I felt God was leading me to move to Atlanta, that I was called to be under the leadership of Bishop Long. He gave me his blessings and I continued to stream. Recina, my son, and I traveled to Lithonia to attend the New Year's Eve service at New Birth. It felt right and that Sunday I joined; I became an official member of New Birth Missionary Baptist Church. My pastor and spiritual father was truly Bishop Eddie L. Long. Later, in February I returned there to take my new member's class, and my son and I had our pictures taken for the membership database. I felt so at home and comfortable.

I returned to Illinois with the intention of getting ready to move. In my preparation I found an apartment home online and filled out the paperwork. Cina's new boyfriend, who also joined the day I did, was preparing to make the same move. I searched but was unable to find a job online. In my mind I was used to having a job. . . and not living by faith. If God says move, obedience is what one needs to do. That wasn't easy for me. Thoughts about my son and how I had to provide for him and myself swept over me; without a job I couldn't do that! I would be moving with no family for a backup plan.

Without realizing it, I just counted God out. I even said to the Lord *If my son were in college and I had a job, I would not have a problem picking up and moving – because I can get a job. I have many skills and it wouldn't be a problem – but to move without a job and with having a child, I'd better wait!* SMH (shaking my head) God Almighty knows all things.

I was not walking by faith or trusting God. He knew I had a child to take care of. He gave him to me. My purpose is to live and walk by faith, and I failed that test at that time. So, the door closed. I was disappointed with myself for not trusting God enough to move by faith.

One of my sisters and I went to visit a church a few miles away, and that particular Sunday the pastors weren't there, but the lady that sang and brought the Word (can I say) was "off the chain"! Elder Antoinette made my soul happy; my spirit leaped with joy, for the Word came to life! It was powerful! This little church reminded me of New Birth. I didn't want to visit too often because I still planned to move to Atlanta; just didn't know when. The next time I visited I did hear the pastor and the co-pastor. They were amazing speakers with fire and power as well. This church, a few miles away, was an extension of a big church house about an hour away from MTV.

I was still streaming all New Birth services and would go to conferences when I was able. Occasionally, I'd visit the POC church with my sisters (who by now had joined). One day my youngest sister asked me to ride with her to a town about 40 minutes away, to accompany their pastor and co-pastor to the Christian TV station. I first said, "No." I had work to do and I told her I didn't want to be around pastors. She assured me we were riding separately. I agreed to go, and took my laptop along so I could do some work. When we met up at the pre-chosen spot, my sister introduced me. Then the pastor said, "Come on and ride with us." My heart dropped, and I told my sister, "See, this is why I didn't want to ride." I swallowed my feelings and got in their car.

It was a pleasant ride and we talked. I answered questions but was careful with what I shared. When we left the television station, the pastor wanted to go to dinner, which we did. As we talked, I became more comfortable and shared more about myself. The pastor suggested I read this book "Making Peace With Your Past," promising to send me a copy if I promised to read it. He did send the book; it was a great book and it helped me. I asked God why was I around pastors and leadership again? Something I was trying my best to avoid. All I could say was "Okay, what are You teaching me, Lord?"

One night the pastor of that church announced that God told him to move to MTV. In obeying God, church services were held at a hotel until they got space at the city airport. Since I had not made my move, I became a member (temporarily) until I could get to Atlanta. Services were powerful! One Sunday Elder Antoinette was ministering and praying for people; and when she prayed for me, I had a breakthrough deliverance. I still needed to let go of my feelings for leaders, pastors, and preachers. I had more layers to remove; on this day I was freed and, on my way, to being made whole. I thank her to this day for allowing God to use her to help me.

Chapter 7

Another Exodus

Lotus & Dianthus Caryophyllus Flowers (God's Flower)
Represent Strength, Resilience & Rebirth

Exodus to the New Destiny Beginning

By 2011 my son graduated HS and was off to college, and eventually I would be making plans for my next move in life. I was still attending POC and serving in various ministries. Media ministry was new to me; I learned about the cameras for streaming, running the lyrics on the screens, and other functions in production. This ministry work would pay off years later.

In 2013, my goddaughter Camille, my middle sister Dillae and I attended a Supernatural Conference at New Birth. While there, I got a Word from the Lord telling me it was time to move. I knew in my spirit it was time so, I started preparing. One Sunday, while serving in the media ministry I felt in my belly (center of my spirit) to tell Bishop Phil, it was time for me to leave and move to Atlanta.

While the youth pastor and I were talking, again I felt the unction; and she told me to go then and tell him. I obeyed, saying to Bishop Phil, "I need to tell you something." When he inquired as to what it was that I needed to tell him, I said: "I had to go and that it was time for me to leave and go to Bishop Long." He said he knew I always wanted to go, and he released me with his blessings. I was just to let him know when and they would send me off in prayer and with his and the co-pastor's blessing. Immediately, I felt a release in my spirit. . . the peace of God that was unexplainable.

I was overseeing a bottled water business for two elderly friends, Patty and her husband, Ron (the assignment mentioned earlier). One day, Ron called me and said Patty had had an aneurysm in her face and was in the hospital, in critical condition. He asked if I would run their business for them because they had no one else; I agreed to do so. Later, Patty got better but didn't want to return to work. So, I continued running their business until 2014, when it was sold.

Upon my return from Atlanta in 2013, I told Ron and Patty that God told me it was time to move to Atlanta. Ron said they would have to sell the business and get a buyer, and that it would take a while. He asked when I was moving, and I said immediately, or as soon as I found a place to live. He began to tell me that it sometimes takes months to sell; and I said (in so many words) to Ron: "God has a buyer, and you will sell. . . because God said I had to go ..." it was time to leave...

Ron started making calls to other franchises. I got reports prepared. The first buyer made an offer in less than 30 days. . . and the offer was accepted. I tell you that God always works on our behalf when we walk in obedience. The purchasers of the business also paid me to help them transition the customers and all the assets. The one other employee also stayed on until he moved back to Florida.

In May 2014, I attended another conference at New Birth but this time, I went to find my new home. When we weren't in sessions, Camille and I would go looking for my home. I didn't know where, but I had searched the Internet and found some apartments close to the church; with having night blindness, I needed to be close by.

We went to one place and the sign said 'Open', but the door was locked. Camille said "Ma, this isn't the one. . . this is a sign; it says 'Open', but the door is locked. . . so it's not the one for you." On we went to the next place, which was a nice, gated community. I met a young man there and told him what I was looking for, and he showed me the model home, which I liked. He asked if I wanted to apply, and I said "Yes." "Where are you from?" was his next question and I replied, "Illinois." Then he asked, "What brings you to Georgia?" I said, "God." I told him I would be attending New Birth and God told me to move; and here I am. He said, "Wow! That is awesome, I've never heard a reason like yours." After filling out the application, I was approved without a payment, and without a job. The deposit was due within a week; rent was due when I moved.

OBEDIENCE, TRUST & FAITH. I walked by faith, obeyed God and trusted the Holy Spirit's guidance. I moved to Lithonia, GA, June 7, 2014.

The Journey continues... stay tuned.

A flower girl is young, innocent and displayed during a happy occasion. Some flower girls are hidden behind secrets and lies, to later be unhidden and revealed as a child of the Most High, God Almighty.

Epilogue

True Forgiveness 41 Years Later

Earlier, I said I forgave my dad, but still didn't know how I would feel if I saw him face to face. Well, it happened on October 21, 2021. My youngest sister suggested we go see our dad and without hesitation, I said "Yes." It was time for me to come face to face with *the boogieman* of my past, the one who had taken me from my bed at night, raped me, and then threatened to harm me, even kill me, (so I thought), if I told anyone. He was the one who stole my identity, then inflicted fear upon me and my siblings.

This person did me wrong! But now it was time to finish my assignment and witness the miraculous power and gift of forgiveness in action. There's nothing like seeing the demons of your past whether in the form of a person, a drink, a place, or drugs. Memories of the past can flood your mind and even cause you to revert to old ways, old thoughts; but I was determined to follow the plan God had laid out for me.

I made all the travel arrangements and we stopped to sightsee and visit other relatives before going on to see our dad. We landed, picked up the rental car, checked into the hotel, and then went in search of our dad. It had been over 35 years since my sisters had seen him, over 41 for me. This was definitely going to be a huge surprise.

We put the address into the GPS and started on our way. I was driving, and even though there was some uncertainty, I still had peace. . . a little nervousness, but not too bad. Again, I prayed, and I knew God was in control; that His Word was true no matter what.

We arrived at the apartment complex, got out of the car, and began looking for his apartment number. We walked around and could see that the building numbers were a bit helter-skelter, going up and down. Walking around the last building, we discovered the numbers went up and down for each apartment very confusing. We walked down a little further and looked up, and there was the apartment. The porch light was off, so we used our phone flashlight to make sure we were in the right place. Dillae was first, I was second, the baby girl (Lol) was behind me recording. . . we wanted to get it all on tape. We were actually really excited!

Dillae knocked on the door and when the door opened there stood our dad. Dillae, smiling and laughing, announced herself, then said, "Here's Joy and Cheech." He was so shocked *and* happy! He hugged Dillae, then me and then his baby girl, Cheech. Now, he has always been a comedian and began cracking 'fat jokes' about us, but admitted he was in disbelief, and his heart was beating fast! It was living proof, finally, that God is truly God Almighty. *Agape love* - God's love - is so real. I had no ill feelings, no pain, only love in my heart for our dear dad.

We spent three days with him going places, eating, taking pictures, and just talking. He loves to talk about Jesus and discipling others. No longer was he 'the boogie man'; this was a changed man, and all I could see was the man God had changed. This is due to his willingness to surrender and become a man of God and live out God's original intent for his life. We had talked often on the phone but seeing him face to face was the proof I needed.

I was truly healed of my past; and this was just what I needed to seal my forgiveness: truth. I know there is a Great God! I truly saw the manifestation of a miracle and deliverance in both our lives.

Forgiveness is of God. And I can say, "God is good, and God is great!" I give Him thanks and I praise His Holy Name today and always.

Again, a flower girl is young and innocent and displayed during a happy occasion. Some flower girls are hidden behind secrets and lies, to later be unhidden and revealed as a child of the Most High, God Almighty.

Try Jesus!!!

I try walking in obedience now, always listening for the voice of God. Before, and without hesitation, I always believed for others that God would answer prayer and manifest His promises but didn't believe for myself. I'd say things like "I know He will do it for you. He may not do it for me, but He will for you." It took me years to learn how to trust God and believe God for myself.

There is a place in our inner man that only God can satisfy. It was put there, I believe, when He breathed into man and man became a living soul. No material thing, no drugs, alcohol, or things of the flesh can satisfy the void in the soul, only God. Jesus is truly the answer and without receiving Jesus as Lord and Savior in and over our lives, we will remain empty and lost.

Read & meditate these Scriptures Romans 10:8-10, 13 (AMP).

8 But what does it say? "The word is near you, in your mouth and in your heart"—that is, the word [the message, the basis] of faith which we preach— 9because if you acknowledge *and* confess with your mouth that Jesus is Lord [recognizing His power, authority, and majesty as God], and believe in your heart that God raised Him from the dead, you will be saved. 10For with the heart a person believes [in Christ as Savior]

resulting in his justification [that is, being made righteous—being freed of the guilt of sin and made acceptable to God]; and with the mouth he acknowledges *and* confesses [his faith openly], resulting in *and* confirming [his] salvation.

¹³ For "whoever calls on the name of the Lord [in prayer] will be saved."

If you are not saved, today is the day for accepting Jesus into your life and making Him Lord over your life. Jesus loves you; God loves you and wants to have a relationship with you.

Repent (turn from your sinful way of life), confess with your mouth, believe in your heart Jesus died for your sins. He was buried, and God raised Him from the dead. Pray and ask Jesus to come into your heart and be Lord over your life.

I won't tell you that trials and tribulations won't come your way, they will; but with Jesus you can overcome and have peace and joy while going through. Once you are saved, get into a good, Bible- teaching church assembly and grow in *God.*

Facts About Incest and Family

- 1/3 to ½ of approximately 150,000 cases of child sexual abuse are committed by a family member in the U.S. each year.
- It is known that at least 1 in 4 girls and 1 in 7 boys are sexually assaulted before the age of 18, with an over-whelming number of these incidents occurring within the family.
- The dynamics of secrecy keep children isolated, away from others and feeling guilty and helpless.
- The legal definition of child sexual abuse usually requires 2 elements: 1) Sexual activities involving a child, 2) An "abusive condition."
- Abusive conditions exist when: the child's partner has a large age or maturational advantage over the child; or the child's partner is in a position of authority or is a care-taker; or the activities are carried out against the child using force or trickery.
- Noncontact sexual abuse usually include exhibitionism, voyeurism, involving a child in watching pornography.
- Child sex abusers fall into 3 main categories: Family, Acquaintances, Strangers
- Children are most vulnerable to sexual abuse between the ages of 7 and 13.
- Retrospective surveys conducted when sexual abuse vic-tims are adults indicate that 10-30% are strangers.

- Between 33-50% of perpetrators who sexually abuse girls are family members.
- 10-20% of those who sexually abuse boys are from within the victim's family.
- Intrafamily abuse continues over a longer period of time than sexual abuse outside the family.
- Parent-child incest can have serious and lasting consequences.
- 20% of all victims develop serious long-term psychological problems which can include: post-traumatic stress disorder, Chronic states of arousal, Nightmares and flashbacks, Anxiety over sex.

REFERENCES

Child Sexual Abuse. (2011, November 29). Retrieved from The National Center for Victims of Crime: NCVC.Org

Davis, S. (2022, April 25). *Incest: The Secret No One Should Keep.* Retrieved from Sexual Abuse: cptsdfoundation.org

Finkelher, D. (1994). Current Information on the Scope and Nature of Child Sexual Abuse. *The Future of Children*

Kluft, Richard P., M. P. (2011, January 12). *Ramifications of Incest.* Retrieved from Psychiatric Times: www.psychiatrictimes.com

Scott, E. (2017, July 12). *How to Become a Safe Place for Your Children.* Retrieved from Renewed Hope Parenting: http://www.renewedhopeparenting.com

U.S. National Library of Medicine (2011). National Institute of Health. *Medline Plus: Child Sexual Abuse.*

About The Author

Joyce Jean Moore is born a native of Mt. Vernon, Illinois. She attended AIU in Chicago, IL where she received her Associate Degree in Business Administration, Bachelor Degree in Information Technology and a Master's Degree in Business Administration/Accounting. She is the owner/CEO of Kingdom Financial Services Management, LLC located in Atlanta, GA, where she has lived for the past 9 years. She is a teacher, mentor, and successful entrepreneur.

Ms. Moore is the proud birth mother of one son and a "mother" to many spiritual sons & daughters. As a born-again believer her greatest joy is her personal relationship with the Lord Jesus, her Friend and Savior.

Consequently, Joy went through many years of abuse until deliverance came and her silence was broken. The Lord intervened, she found her voice, and began to tell her story. He made a way of escape, and she began her journey to wholeness and victory.

Unfortunately, Joy's story is the story of several little girls and even little boys. Perhaps, this is your story, or you know of someone who is in an abusive home. Hopefully, as you read the details of Joy's story, you will find your voice, as well as a safe place (friend, neighbor, relative, teacher, pastor) to speak and tell your story too, so that you can be rescued from your situation whether past or present. Don't lose hope and don't give up! There is help for your situation.

(See additional information)

Additional Information

Sexual Assault Hotline: Free & Confidential 24/7. 800-656-4673 (800-656-HOPE)

Rape, Abuse, and Incest National Network: 800-656-4673

National Child Abuse Hotline (24 Hour):
800-4-A-Child or 800-422-4453

National Suicide Prevention Lifeline:
800-273-8255